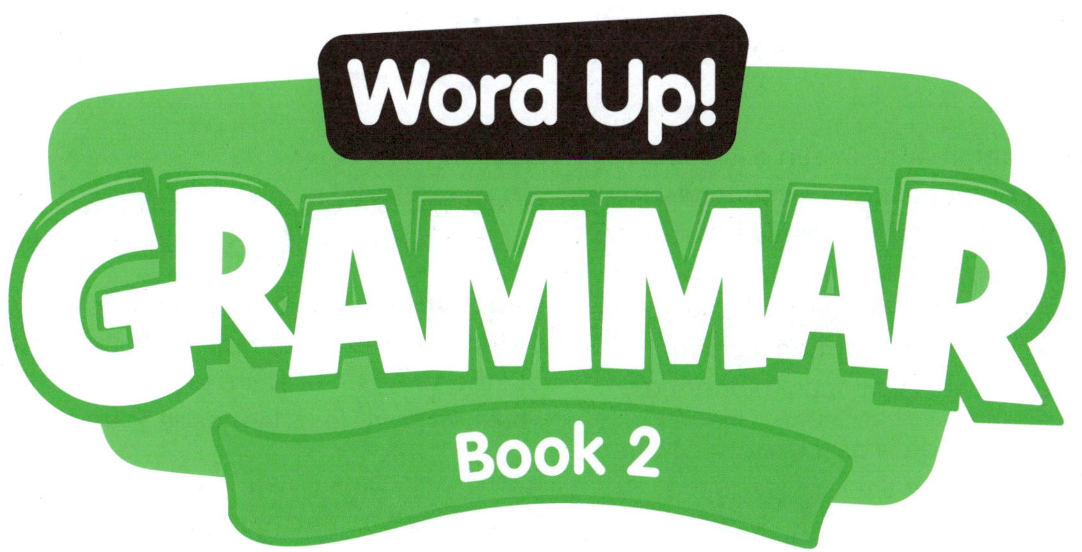

Kerry Shanahan

Why Do We Need **Word Up!**?

Word Up! Grammar has been designed in response to an identified classroom need – the need for a differentiated student activity book series linked to the national curriculum. Each unit makes explicit links to the Australian Curriculum content descriptions, general capabilities and cross-curriculum priorities.

Grammar knowledge is best expanded when integrated with other areas of language. **Word Up!** promotes listening, speaking, reading and writing through a diverse range of open and closed activities. The series builds on grammar skills sequentially. Each skill is introduced through varied and engaging texts that stimulate critical and imaginative thinking.

What's in it for teachers?

Word Up! Grammar is a flexible and dynamic student activity series anchored by a sound learning scope and sequence. The book demonstrates how grammar features and structures work at a word, sentence and text level. Grammar is practised and assessed through multimodal, traditional and everyday text.

Each book contains 25 four-page units of work. We recommend integrating one unit per week with your current literacy program. Each unit introduces one or two grammar skills in simple language supported by examples.

What's in it for students?

Topics are broad and level-specific. The series engages students by showing them how grammar lives and breathes in their world.

Through the series, students discover figurative speech through colourful lyric poetry, build expressive noun groups in the lost world of folktales and learn the art of persuasion through modal verbs and emotive language.

Series overview

Word Up! Lower (books 1 and 2) has a special focus on visual literacy for younger learners.

Word Up! Middle and Upper (books 3–6) include annotated sample texts that point out the structure of each text type and, where relevant, point to its language features.

Each book also contains a Scope and Sequence map and a Glossary.

Because we're all different …

Each **Word Up! Grammar** unit defines the skill, provides examples, models answers and paces activities. Key grammar skills are revised and built on from unit to unit. All students access learning through gradually increasing levels of difficulty. The level of support decreases as students progress through learning and practice.

Differentiated student learning is indicated by three icons:

 indicates basic, closed activities with a high level of student support

 indicates a moderate level of student support, with a mix of closed and open activity types

 indicates student-led activities that are writing-centred and open-response

Students can follow the **Word Up!** silly spider through each unit. When students have completed all units, they receive a Certificate of Completion at the end of the book.

What's in a Unit?

Unit icons
Indicate the question type and level of difficulty

Unit anchor
Defines the "skill in focus" and provides examples

Sunshine activites
Basic, closed questions with extra student support

Unit 1 **The Great Race**

A **proper noun** is the name of a person, place or thing. *Mary, Darwin* and *December* are examples of proper nouns. A proper noun begins with a capital letter.

When two or more people talk to each other it is called a **dialogue**. Plays have dialogue between characters.

Play

The Great Race

Characters:
• Fred, a fish • Pete, a platypus • Lucy, a lizard

Scene 1: The challenge

Fred: Who wants to race to Rocky Island?

Pete: I will. I'm a great swimmer.

Lucy: Me too. I'll beat you both.

Fred: Don't be silly, Lucy! You can't even swim.

Scene 2: The race

Pete: Ready. Set. Go!

Lucy: I'll make a boat out of a leaf. I will win the race.

Scene 3: The winner

Lucy: Hi, Fred. Hi, Pete. I told you I'd win!

10

1 Circle the proper nouns in the play.

2 Write the characters' names from the play. Remember to use capital letters for proper nouns.

3 Write a sentence of dialogue that Pete says in the play and a sentence that Lucy says.

4 Find the proper nouns in the word search.

Adelaide March Sara Jason Bendigo Arun

A	d	e	l	a	i	d	e
r	o	g	i	d	n	e	B
u	p	S	a	r	a	q	a
n	J	a	s	o	n	t	i
M	a	r	c	h	a	f	m
t	s	a	b	f	v	h	o

Adelaide

11

Text type sample
Short texts provide a learning context

Moon activities
Closed and open questions

Lightning bolt activities
Student-led, writing-centred, open-response activities

5 Tick the sentences that are examples of dialogue. Remember that dialogue is when two or more people talk to one another.

a I am not at school today because it is Saturday.

b Caterina: Simon, can I have my bag please?

c Kevin: Mum, I am wearing my red jumper.

d Three pigs walked across the farmyard.

6 Circle the proper nouns.

today	Pete	hello
Monday	go	Fred
Lucy	Rocky Island	school

7 Write a proper noun for each category. An example of each has been done for you.

Days of the week	Months of the year	Planets in the solar system
Monday	January	Mercury

8 Rewrite the sentences using capital letters for proper nouns.

a susan had her piano exam in may.

b dominic sent a letter from new south wales to a friend.

12

c michael's birthday is in the month of september.

9 Write your own short play. Remember to use dialogue and proper nouns.

Play title:

Characters:

Scene 1:

Scene 2:

13

Scope and Sequence

Unit	Unit title	Page	Text / text type	Text and sentence grammar skill	Word level grammar skill	Focus on
1	**The Great Race**	10	Play	Dialogue	Proper nouns	E.g. Mary, Darwin, December
2	**My Cousins in China**	14	Diary	Simple sentences	Capital letters Proper nouns	E.g. Mitch and Ruby went to China.
3	**The Koala Trail**	18	Personal recount	Simple past tense	Proper nouns	E.g. Caitlin went to Raymond Island.
4	**A Yabby Home**	22	Instructions	Numbered sequence of actions	Conjunctions	E.g. and, but, because, or
5	**Super Spiders**	26	Information report	Use of dot points	Commas	E.g. crickets, beetles, caterpillars
6	**Living in Groups**	30	Website	Indirect speech	Collective nouns	E.g. hive, colony, pride, troop, school
7	**Playground Survey**	34	Survey	Topic sentences	Present tense verbs Articles	E.g. play, use, do, are, show E.g. a, an, the
8	**A Day on the Reef**	38	Diary	Indirect speech	Pronouns	E.g. I, you, he, she, it, we, they

	Australian Curriculum content descriptions*	General capabilities / cross-curriculum priorities*	Learning areas*
	Recognise that capital letters signal proper nouns and commas are used to separate items in lists *(ACELA1465)* Also: *ACELA1463, ACELA1468*	• Literacy • Critical and creative thinking	English
	Recognise that capital letters signal proper nouns and commas are used to separate items in lists *(ACELA1465)* Also: *ACELA1463, ACELA1468*	• Literacy • Critical and creative thinking • Intercultural understanding • Asia and Australia's engagement with Asia	English Geography
	Understand that nouns represent people, places, things and ideas and can be, for example, common, proper, concrete and abstract, and that noun groups can be expanded using articles and adjectives *(ACELA1468)* Also: *ACELA1465, ACELY1671*	• Literacy • Critical and creative thinking • ICT competence	English Geography
	Understand that simple connections can be made between ideas by using a compound sentence with two or more clauses and coordinating conjunctions *(ACELA1467)* Also: *ACELA1463, ACELY1671*	• Literacy • Critical and creative thinking • Numeracy • Sustainability • Personal and social competence	English Maths Science
	Recognise that capital letters signal proper nouns and commas are used to separate items in lists *(ACELA1465)* Also: *ACELY1671, ACELA1463*	• Literacy • Numeracy • Sustainability • Critical and creative thinking • ICT competence	English Maths Science
	Know some features of text organisation including page and screen layouts, alphabetical order, and different types of diagrams, for example timelines *(ACELA1466)* Also: *ACELA1470, ACELY1671*	• Literacy • Critical and creative thinking • Sustainability • ICT competence	English Science
	Understand that different types of texts have identifiable text structures and language features that help the text serve its purpose *(ACELA1463)* Also: *ACELA1470, ACELA1468*	• Literacy • Critical and creative thinking • Numeracy • Personal and social competence	English Maths
	Understand the use of vocabulary about familiar and new topics and experiment with and begin to make conscious choices of vocabulary to suit audience and purpose *(ACELA1470)* Also: *ACELA1468, ACELY1669*	• Literacy • Critical and creative thinking • Numeracy • Sustainability	English Maths Science

**Source:* Australian Curriculum

Unit	Unit title	Page	Text / text type	Text and sentence grammar skill	Word level grammar skill	Focus on
9	**Read All About It!**	42	Newspaper report	Chronological list of events	Noun groups and number adjectives Articles	E.g. first, second, third E.g. a, an, the
10	**Coin Cleaner**	46	Experiment	Vocabulary used for an experiment	Technical nouns	E.g. equipment, procedure, results, aim
11	**There Once Was …**	50	Limericks	Sentence structure in poetry (limerick)	Action verbs Rhyming words	E.g. cry, skate, run, search, learn, sleep
12	**Barry Bunny**	54	Narrative: rhyme	Sequence of events	Antonyms	E.g. tough / gentle, weak / strong
13	**Frog Princess**	58	Fairytale	Compound sentences	Conjunctions	E.g. and, or, but, so, yet
14	**Hopscotch**	62	Game instructions	Numbered sequence of actions	Connectives	E.g. first, then, to begin, next, now, however
15	**Cinquains**	66	Cinquains	Syllables in a line of poetry	Synonyms	E.g. fierce / strong, stalking / creeping
16	**All About Nature**	70	Haiku	Descriptive language in poetry	Describing adjectives Number adjectives	E.g. three fast, new, shiny cars
17	**Planting Day**	74	Advertisement	Statements of fact and opinion	Exclamation marks	E.g. I went to the movies. I love the movies!

	Australian Curriculum content descriptions*	General capabilities / cross-curriculum priorities*	Learning areas*
	Understand that nouns represent people, places, things and ideas and can be, for example, common, proper, concrete and abstract, and that noun groups can be expanded using articles and adjectives *(ACELA1468)* Also: *ACELA1463, ACELY1671*	• Literacy • Critical and creative thinking • Numeracy • Personal and social competence	English Maths
	Understand that different types of texts have identifiable text structures and language features that help the text serve its purpose *(ACELA1463)* Also: *ACELA1468, ACELA1470*	• Literacy • Critical and creative thinking • Numeracy	English Maths Science
	Identify, reproduce and experiment with rhythmic, sound and word patterns in poems, chants, rhymes and songs *(ACELT1592)* Also: *ACELA1463, ACELY1671*	• Literacy • Critical and creative thinking • Numeracy	English Maths
	Understand how texts are made cohesive through resources, for example word associations, synonyms, and antonyms *(ACELA1464)* Also: *ACELT1592, ACELA1469*	• Literacy • Critical and creative thinking • Personal and social competence	English
	Understand that simple connections can be made between ideas by using a compound sentence with two or more clauses and coordinating conjunctions *(ACELA1467)* Also: *ACELY1671, ACELA1463*	• Literacy • Critical and creative thinking	English
	Understand how texts are made cohesive through resources, for example word associations, synonyms, and antonyms *(ACELA1464)* Also: *ACELY1666, ACELY1671*	• Literacy • Critical and creative thinking • Numeracy • Personal and social competence	English Maths
	Identify, reproduce and experiment with rhythmic, sound and word patterns in poems, chants, rhymes and songs *(ACELT1592)* Also: *ACELA1463, ACELA1464*	• Literacy • Critical and creative thinking • Numeracy	English Maths
	Identify, reproduce and experiment with rhythmic, sound and word patterns in poems, chants, rhymes and songs *(ACELT1592)* Also: *ACELA1470, ACELY1671*	• Literacy • Critical and creative thinking • Numeracy • Intercultural understanding • Asia and Australia's engagement with Asia	English Maths
	Identify the audience of imaginative, informative and persuasive texts *(ACELY1668)* Also: *ACELA1463, ACELY1671*	• Literacy • Critical and creative thinking • Personal and social competence • Sustainability	English Science

****Source:** Australian Curriculum*

Unit	Unit title	Page	Text / text type	Text and sentence grammar skill	Word level grammar skill	Focus on
18	**The Canoe Tree**	78	Explanation	Questioning sentences	Question marks	E.g. What is a canoe tree?
19	**Going Green**	82	Newspaper report	Statements of fact	Past tense verbs	E.g. planted, used, made, said, was, were
20	**Feed Me!**	86	Venn diagram	Precise language	Concrete nouns	E.g. ice, song, car, juice, bread
21	**My Eyes**	90	Explanation	Use of diagrams to explain written information	Adverbs used to describe where, when and how	E.g. immediately, quickly, happily, yesterday, often, never
22	**Sandcastles**	94	Story	Direct speech	Synonyms and antonyms	E.g. sad / upset E.g. young / old
23	**The Letter Hunt**	98	Directions	Commands	Conjunctions	E.g. because, and, or, but, so, yet
24	**My Dad, the Hero**	102	Book review	Sentences of opinion	Present tense and present continuous	E.g. is, asks, give; I am laughing.
25	**The Class Party**	106	Invitation	Emotive language	Abstract nouns	E.g. friendship, excitement, pleasure, fun, joy, happiness

	Australian Curriculum content descriptions*	General capabilities / cross-curriculum priorities*	Learning areas*
	Understand the use of vocabulary about familiar and new topics and experiment with and begin to make conscious choices of vocabulary to suit audience and purpose *(ACELA1470)* Also: *ACELY1668, ACELY1671*	• Literacy • Critical and creative thinking • Intercultural understanding • Aboriginal and Torres Strait Islander histories and cultures • History	English History
	Understand that different types of texts have identifiable text structures and language features that help the text serve its purpose *(ACELA1463)* Also: *ACELA1470, ACELY1671*	• Literacy • Critical and creative thinking • Intercultural understanding • Personal and social competence • Ethical behaviour • Aboriginal and Torres Strait Islander histories and cultures • Sustainability	English History
	Understand that nouns represent people, places, things and ideas and can be, for example, common, proper, concrete and abstract, and that noun groups can be expanded using articles and adjectives *(ACELA1468)* Also: *ACELA1466, ACELY1671*	• Literacy • Critical and creative thinking • Numeracy	English Maths Science
	Know some features of text organisation including page and screen layouts, alphabetical order, and different types of diagrams, for example timelines *(ACELA1466)* Also: *ACELA1463, ACELY1671*	• Literacy • Critical and creative thinking • Sustainability	English Science Geography
	Understand how texts are made cohesive through resources, for example word associations, synonyms, and antonyms *(ACELA1464)* Also: *ACELA1463, ACELY1671*	• Literacy • Critical and creative thinking • Ethical behaviour • Personal and social competence	English
	Listen for specific purposes and information, including instructions, and extend students' own and others' ideas in discussions *(ACELY1666)* Also: *ACELA1467, ACELY1661*	• Literacy • Critical and creative thinking • Numeracy • Personal and social competence	English Maths
	Identify language that can be used for appreciating texts and the qualities of people and things *(ACELA1462)* Also: *ACELY1668, ACELY1661*	• Literacy • Critical and creative thinking • Intercultural understanding • Asia and Australia's engagement with Asia • Personal and social competence	English
	Understand that nouns represent people, places, things and ideas and can be, for example, common, proper, concrete and abstract, and that noun groups can be expanded using articles and adjectives *(ACELA1468)* Also: *ACELA1470, ACELY1671*	• Literacy • Critical and creative thinking	English

**Source:* Australian Curriculum*

Unit 1

The Great Race

A **proper noun** is the name of a person, place or thing. *Mary*, *Darwin* and *December* are examples of proper nouns. A proper noun begins with a capital letter.

When two or more people talk to each other it is called a **dialogue**. Plays have dialogue between characters.

Play

The Great Race

Characters:

- Fred, a fish
- Pete, a platypus
- Lucy, a lizard

Scene 1: The challenge

Fred: Who wants to race to Rocky Island?

Pete: I will. I'm a great swimmer.

Lucy: Me too. I'll beat you both.

Fred: Don't be silly, Lucy!
You can't even swim.

Scene 2: The race

Pete: Ready. Set. Go!

Lucy: I'll make a boat out of a leaf. I will win the race.

Scene 3: The winner

Lucy: Hi, Fred. Hi, Pete. I told you I'd win!

1 Circle the proper nouns in the play.

2 Write the characters' names from the play. Remember to use capital letters for proper nouns.

3 Write a sentence of dialogue that Pete says in the play and a sentence that Lucy says.

4 Find the proper nouns in the word search.

Adelaide March Sara Jason Bendigo Arun

A	d	e	l	a	i	d	e
r	o	g	i	d	n	e	B
u	p	S	a	r	a	q	a
n	J	a	s	o	n	t	i
M	a	r	c	h	a	f	m
t	s	a	b	f	v	h	o

5 Tick the sentences that are examples of dialogue. Remember that dialogue is when two or more people talk to one another.

a I am not at school today because it is Saturday.

b Caterina: Simon, can I have my bag please?

c Kevin: Mum, I am wearing my red jumper.

d Three pigs walked across the farmyard.

6 Circle the proper nouns.

today	Pete	hello
Monday	go	Fred
Lucy	Rocky Island	school

7 Write a proper noun for each category. An example of each has been done for you.

Days of the week	Months of the year	Planets in the solar system
Monday	January	Mercury

8 Rewrite the sentences using capital letters for proper nouns.

a susan had her piano exam in may.

____

b dominic sent a letter from new south wales to a friend.

____

c michael's birthday is in the month of september.

9 **Write your own short play. Remember to use dialogue and proper nouns.**

Play title:

Characters:

Scene 1:

Scene 2:

Unit 2

My Cousins in China

A **simple sentence** is a sentence with one main idea or message. This is a simple sentence: *I am going home.*

A **proper noun** is the name of a person, place or thing.

Capital letters are used at the beginning of a sentence and for proper nouns.

Diary

Saturday 29 April

Today I spoke to Mitch and Ruby. They are my cousins. They went to live in China in February. I spoke to them through a video call on the computer. It was exciting to see them and speak to them.

Ruby told me they went to a zoo in China. They saw a huge panda!

Mitch said that China and Australia are very different. He likes living there. So does Ruby.

I told Mitch and Ruby that I miss them. They miss me, too.

Sunday 30 April

Today I wrote a letter to Mitch and Ruby. I added a photo of the three of us together. I will post my letter tomorrow.

1 **Circle the capital letters in the diary.**

2 **Write three proper nouns from the diary.**

3 **Write the first word from each sentence.**

a Ruby told me they went to a zoo in China.

____

b They saw a huge panda! ______________

c Mitch said that China and Australia are very different.

____

4 **Find the proper nouns in the word search.**

Beijing April Bruce Yoshi Broome China

B	e	i	j	i	n	g	e
r	l	A	p	r	i	l	w
u	p	Y	o	s	h	i	a
c	a	t	c	r	a	z	i
e	B	r	o	o	m	e	m
y	d	a	n	i	h	C	k

5 **Write a proper noun for each category. Use the words in the box to help you. Some examples have been done for you.**

Yarra River	Queensland	Mrs Smith
Aiden	Eiffel Tower	South Australia

People	Places	Things
Laura	Alice Springs	Pacific Ocean

6 **Rewrite each sentence as two simple sentences. Remember to use capital letters and full stops correctly.**

a I took my dog to the park and he chased a cat up a tree.

b I went to a party and danced all afternoon.

c First I played soccer and then I played on the playground.

7 Write one simple sentence for each picture. Remember to use capital letters at the start of each sentence and for proper nouns.

a Baxter ______________________________

____

b ______________________________

____

c Atlantic Ocean ______________________________

____

8 Write your own diary entry for a weekend. Include at least three proper nouns. Remember to use capital letters in the correct places.

Saturday

____

____

____

Sunday

____

____

____

Unit 3 The Koala Trail

A **proper noun** is the name of a person, place or thing. *Chan*, *Australia* and *Yarra River* are examples of proper nouns. A proper noun begins with a capital letter.

The **past tense** is used to write about things that have already happened. *I went to the shop. The dog barked.*

Personal Recount

A Day at Raymond Island

During the school holidays, I went to Raymond Island. I went with my sister Caitlin and my grandparents. To get there we drove to a town called Paynesville. We caught a ferry. The ferry runs all day, taking people, cars, buses and bikes to and from the island.

On the island we went for a walk on a koala trail. I counted nine koalas. Most of them were asleep, but Caitlin saw one eating gum leaves.

After lunch, we caught the ferry back to the mainland. Then we drove to Bairnsdale where we were staying for the night.

We had a fantastic time!

1 **Circle the proper nouns in the personal recount.**

2 **Write the proper nouns that are places from the personal recount.**

______________ ______________ ______________

3 **Underline the words that are written in the past tense.**

went	go
walked	walk
stop	stopped
drove	drive
catch	caught
make	made
sat	sit

4 **Find the proper nouns in the word search.**

Rome Hobart Bulla Japan London Spain

B	r	z	s	e	m	o	R
u	H	o	b	a	r	t	s
l	n	n	a	p	a	J	p
l	L	o	n	d	o	n	s
a	o	n	i	a	p	S	t
s	i	l	t	m	n	u	r

5 **Draw a line to match the word to its past tense form. The first one has been done for you.**

a run	saw
b eat	danced
c see	ran
d drink	cleaned
e dance	ate
f clean	drank

6 **Circle a word in each sentence that shows it is written in the past tense. The first one has been done for you.**

a I watched the basketball game.

b My sister played chess with me.

c I ate dinner with my grandma.

d You were the best singer in the concert!

e After dinner I went home.

7 **Fill in the gaps with the correct past tense word. Use the words in the box to help you. The first one has been done for you.**

juggled walked dropped
~~went~~ saw did broke

Last week I went to the circus.

I ______________ a clown. He ______________ some plates.

He ______________ the plates and they ______________.

An acrobat ______________ backflips and ______________

along a tightrope high up in the tent.

8 Write a short personal recount about something fun that you did. Use the past tense and remember to use capital letters correctly. Here are some topics you could write about.

- A day at the zoo
- A day at the beach
- A day at the park

9 Raymond Island is off the coast of Victoria, Australia. Find it on an online map.

Unit 4 A Yabby Home

A **conjunction** is a word that is used to link two ideas in a sentence, such as *and*, *but*, *because* and *or*.
I want to play tennis, but it is raining.
An **instruction** tells us how to make or do something. The steps are numbered so that we do things in the correct order.

Instructions

How to make a yabby home

You will need:

- a glass tank
- small pebbles
- a large rock
- a pump and an air filter
- water plants
- grated carrot
- 2 or 3 yabbies

What to do:

1 Cover the bottom of the glass tank with small pebbles.

2 Put the large rock on top of the pebbles so that the yabbies have somewhere to hide.

3 Ask an adult to help you set up the pump and air filter.

4 Fill the tank with cold water, but not right to the top.

5 Add the water plants and grated carrot, because the yabbies will need some food to eat.

6 Put the yabbies in their home and watch them explore.

1 **Circle the first step in the instructions.**

2 **Underline the third step in the instructions.**

3 **Shade the conjunctions in the instructions in red. Use the words in the box to help you.**

and but because so

4 **Fill in the gaps with the missing conjunctions.**

a Fill the tank with cold water,

_______________ not right to the top.

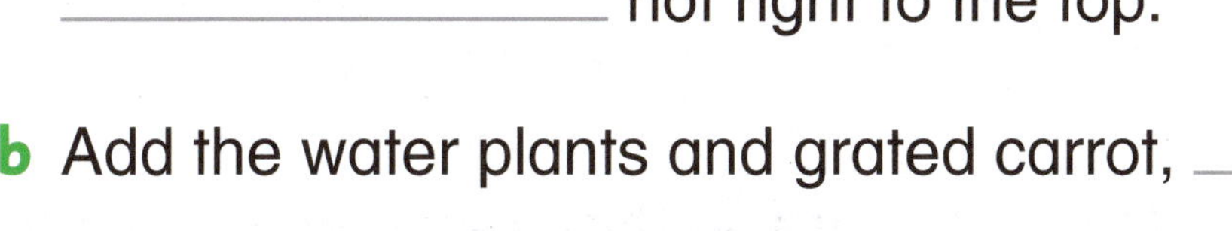

b Add the water plants and grated carrot, _______________ the yabbies will need some food to eat.

c Put the yabbies in their home _______________ watch them explore.

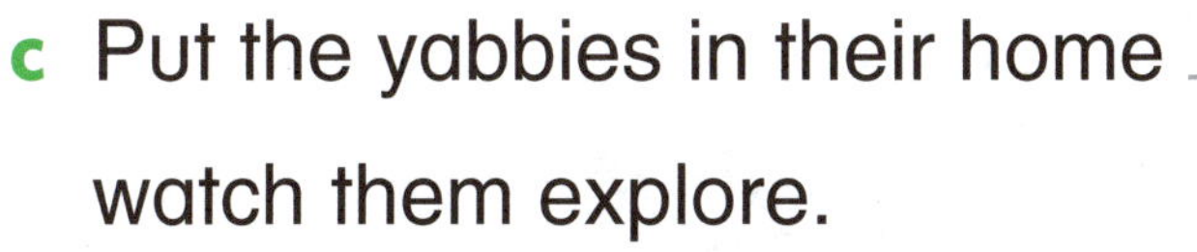

5 **Find the conjunctions in the word search.**

because and but or so

a	n	d	x	w	c	t	c
b	e	s	u	a	c	e	b
d	g	h	k	e	l	t	u
o	r	q	n	m	j	k	t
s	d	v	r	n	o	i	l

6 **Fill in the gaps with the correct conjunctions. Use the words in the box to help you. The first one has been done for you.**

~~because~~	but	and	or

a I was late for school because I missed the bus.

b Marcus wanted to make pancakes, __________ he didn't have any eggs.

c Should I walk to the shops __________ should I ride my bike?

d We are having fish __________ chips for dinner.

7 **Number the steps in the procedure so that the actions are done in the correct order. Use the pictures to help you.**

1 

2 

3 

4 

_______ Lift your dog out of the tub and dry it with a towel.

_______ Place your dog in the tub.

_______ Wash your dog with a soft cloth and rinse the soap off it.

_______ Put warm water in a tub, but don't fill it to the top.

8 **Circle the conjunctions in the sentences.**

a Patrick is good at soccer because he is a fast runner.

b I would love to have a pet fish or bird.

c The cat tried really hard, but it couldn't catch the mouse.

9 **Write your own procedure about how to get ready for school. Remember to use conjunctions.**

How to get ready for school

You will need:

- ______________________
- ______________________
- ______________________
- ______________________

What to do:

____

____

____

____

____

____

Unit 5 Super Spiders

A **comma** (,) is a punctuation mark.

A comma can be used to separate items in a list.

On my farm there are cows, horses, sheep and pigs.

Sometimes a list can be written using **dot points** (•).

Information Report

Super Spiders

All spiders have things in common. They have:

- eight legs
- two body parts
- a skeleton on the outside of their bodies
- strong jaws.

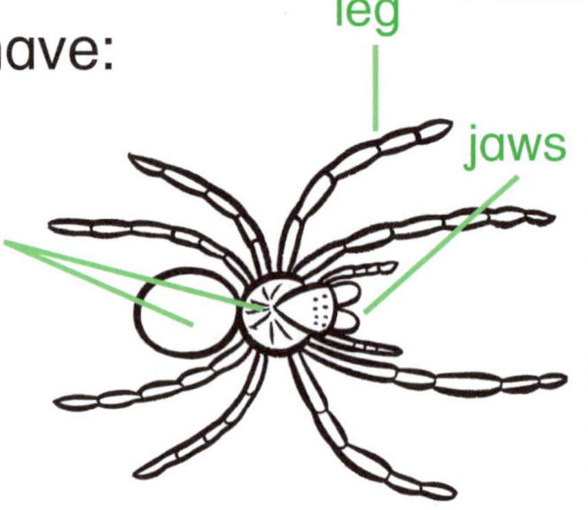

Spiders come in many colours, including black, brown, white, grey, yellow, green and orange.

There are different types of spiders. The red-back spider is a round, black spider. The female has a red stripe on its back.

The funnel-web spider has a dark, shiny body. It has large, powerful fangs.

Tarantulas are big, hairy spiders. Tarantulas eat crickets, grasshoppers, beetles, caterpillars and most other insects.

1 **Circle the commas in the information report.**

2 **Practise writing three commas. Copy the commas below.**

3 **Write the missing dot points in the list. Use the information report to help you. Two examples have been done for you.**

Tarantulas eat:

- crickets
-
-
-
- most other insects.

4 **Add commas to the sentences.**

a The kitten was tiny fluffy cute and snugly.

b I felt scared alone and nervous.

c Max Tran Zac and Will are on my basketball team.

d The funnel-web spider showed its large powerful fangs.

e It was a small shiny fast red car.

f Peas carrots corn and potatoes were on my plate.

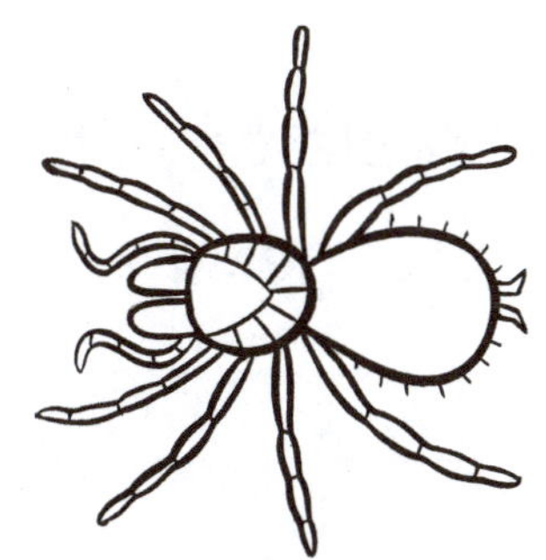

5 Add dot points and commas where they are needed.

For my birthday party I will need:

___ balloons

___ streamers

___ party hats

___ a birthday cake.

I will invite Sam Annika Lisa Liam Josh and Maya.

6 Finish the sentences using the pictures to help you. Remember to use commas and full stops.

a We have three pets. We have ____________

____

b For my birthday I got ____________

____

7 Rewrite these sentences using commas in the correct places.

a My best friends are Ciara and Lexi and Liesl and Amina.

____

b Yesterday I bought an apple and some grapes and an orange.

____

8 Add the commas and dot points to the information report.

Elephants

Elephants have:

four legs

big ears

a large body

a long trunk.

Elephants like to eat many things. They eat plants grasses leaves bark and fruit.

Elephants play in the mud to keep their skin cool. They use their trunks to pick up things reach high branches and put food and water in their mouths.

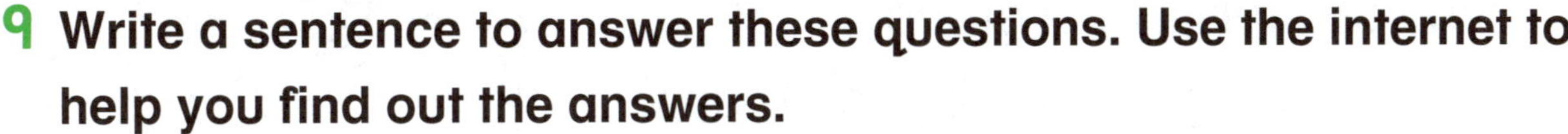

9 Write a sentence to answer these questions. Use the internet to help you find out the answers.

a What do elephants eat? (Write one thing.)

____

b Why do elephants play in mud?

____

c What do elephants use their trunks for? (Write one thing.)

____

Unit 6

Living in Groups

A **collective noun** is a noun that talks about a group of people or things, for example *a bunch of grapes* or *a herd of cattle*.

Indirect speech is used to tell us something that someone has said. It is not quoted in speech marks (“ ”).
Peter told me that he cleaned his shoes.

Website

Home | About | Contacts

Kingdom of Animals

Living in groups

Some animals live in groups.
My teacher says that living in groups helps these animals to survive.

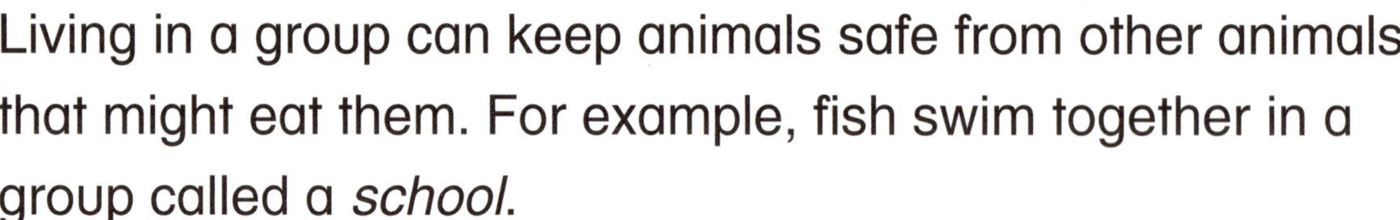

Living in a group can keep animals safe from other animals that might eat them. For example, fish swim together in a group called a *school*.

Some animals live in groups because they help each other to work together. Ants live in a group called a *colony*. Bees live in a group called a *hive*.

My dad says that lions live in a group called a *pride*.

1 **Circle the collective nouns in the text. Use the words in the box to help you.**

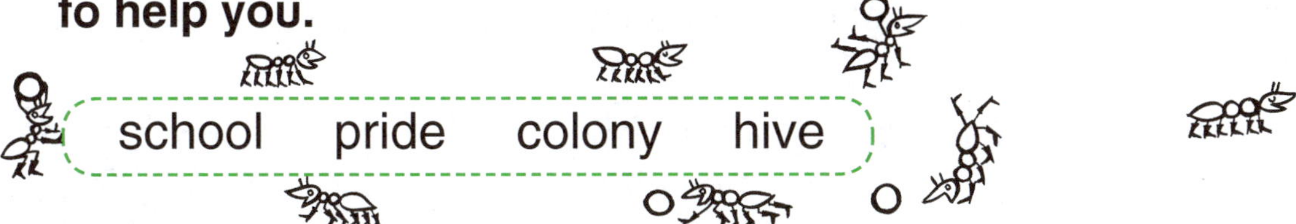

2 **Underline a sentence in the text that is an example of indirect speech. An example has been done for you.**

3 **Fill in the missing collective nouns. Use the text to help you.**

a A group of fish is called a ________________________.

b A group of ants is called a ________________________.

c A group of lions is called a ________________________.

d A group of bees is called a ________________________.

4 **Draw a line to match the collective noun to the group of animals it describes. The first one has been done for you.**

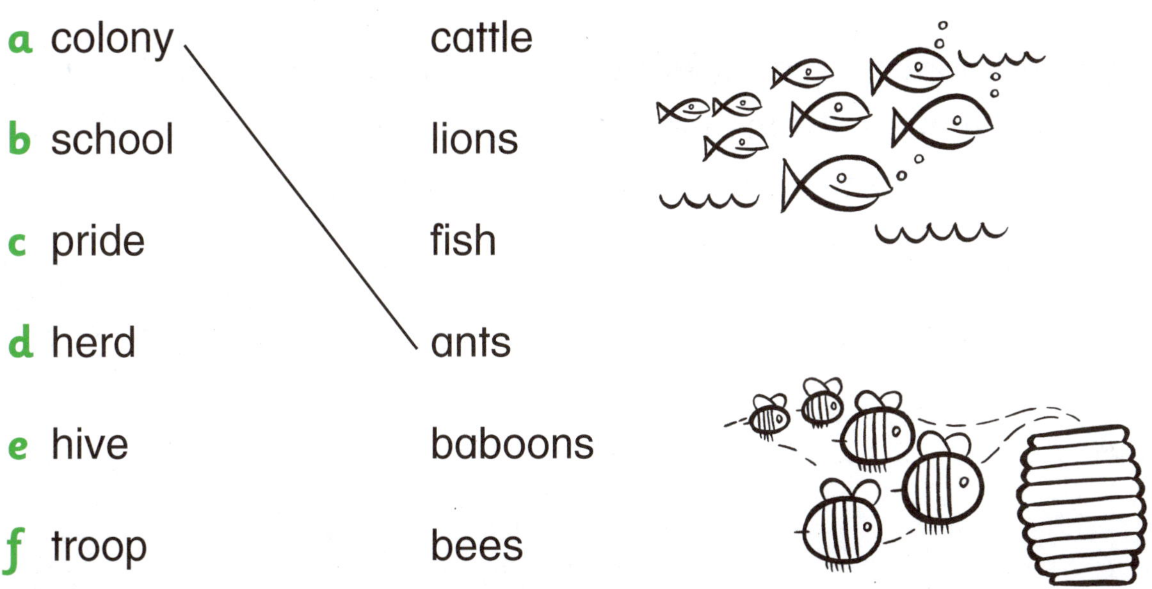

5 **Draw a smiley face next to the sentences that use indirect speech. Remember that indirect speech does not use speech marks (“ ”).**

a “I'll post the letter today,” said Tahlia.

b Tahlia said that she would post the letter today.

c “We have cleaned the floor,” said Jamal and Lucy.

d Jamal and Lucy said that they had cleaned the floor.

6 **Write a collective noun that describes each group. Use the words in the box to help you.**

class choir team

a A group of children at school: ____________________

b A group of basketball players: ____________________

c A group of people singing: ____________________

7 **Fill in the gaps with a collective noun that you think suits each group of animals. Some animals have collective nouns that tell us something about how the animals look, sound or act. Use the words in the box to help you.**

paddling prickle rainbow brood

a A ____________________ of hedgehogs

b A ____________________ of chickens

c A ____________________ of butterflies

d A ______________________ of ducks

8 Write about an animal that lives in a group. Why i group good for this animal?

Unit 7 Playground Survey

A **present tense verb** tells us about an action that is happening now or happens regularly.
The cat eats fish.

A **topic sentence** tells us what a paragraph is about. It is usually at the beginning of a paragraph.

An **article** is a small word that comes before the noun, for example *a boy*, *an apple* or *the lady*.

Survey

The teachers at Sunny Primary School wanted to find out how often the students use the playground. Each student in the school answered a question in a survey.

How often do you play on the playground?

- ☐ Every day
- ☐ 2–3 times a week
- ☐ Once a week
- ☐ Never

Results of the survey show that the students at Sunny Primary School use the playground often. Thirty students use it every day. Fifty students use it 2–3 times a week. Twenty students use it once a week. No students replied that they never use the playground.

1 **Circle the verbs in the survey that are written in the present tense. Use the words in the box to help you.**

do play show use

2 **Underline the topic sentence in the survey. Remember, a topic sentence is usually at the beginning of a paragraph.**

3 **Draw a star above the articles (*a* or *the*) in the survey.**

4 **Write the correct present tense verb below each picture. Use the words in the box to help you.**

run drink laugh skip

5 **Draw a line to match the article to a noun. In some cases, there may be more than one correct answer.**

a an — orange

b the — umbrella

c a — spider

d an — banana

6 **Write the present tense verb for each word. The first one has been done for you.**

a played ___play___

b used ______________

c showed ______________

7 **Fill in the gaps with the correct present tense verbs. Use the words in the box to help you.**

a My sister ______________ with her toys.

b My friends ______________ good at netball.

c I ______________ my homework every day.

d Ants ______________ nests to live in.

8 **Rewrite these sentences in the present tense. The first one has been done for you.**

a I walked home from school.

I walk home from school.

b I talked to my cousin on the phone.

____

c Phillip splashed in the sea.

____

d The waves were huge!

___

9 **Underline the topic sentence in each paragraph.**

a During the school holidays, I went to visit my grandparents. We did lots of fun things. We went to the beach and to the park. We even went to the circus. I love Grandma and Grandpa!

b I am learning to play the piano. I go to lessons every week, and I practise every day. My teacher tells me that I am getting better and better. Soon, I will play in my very first concert.

10 **Survey your friends to find out which foods they like best.**

My Friends' Favourite Foods

Type of food	How many people like it best?
Pizza	
Dumplings	
Fruit salad	
Ice cream	
Carrots	

a How many people like carrots the best? ___

b How many people like fruit salad the best? ___

c Which food is the most popular? ___

Unit 8

A Day on the Reef

A **pronoun** is a word that takes the place of a noun.
<u>Sue</u> ran home. <u>She</u> ran home.
I, *you*, *he*, *she*, *it*, *we* and *they* are examples of pronouns.

Indirect speech is used to tell us something that someone has said. It is not quoted in speech marks (“ ”).
My teacher told me to read.

Diary

Monday 2 August

Dad and I went to the Great Barrier Reef today.

On the boat to the reef we saw four humpback whales. <u>The captain said that there are lots of whales in this part of the ocean.</u>

We went snorkelling at the reef. We saw huge schools of fish. I saw small, big, stripy, fat and thin fish.

We saw lots of coral too. It was awesome! The tour guide said that there are many types of coral on the reef. She pointed out plate coral, brain coral and finger coral.

The Great Barrier Reef is amazing!

1 **Circle the pronouns in the diary. Use the words in the box to help you.**

I we it she

2 **Underline a sentence in the diary that is an example of indirect speech. An example has been done for you.**

3 **Circle the pronouns in the sentences. Use the words in the box to help you.**

I they we you

a I like drawing.

b Are you going to Kosta's party?

c We are having pasta for dinner tonight.

d Eric and Julia are good at basketball. They are good at lots of sports.

4 **Draw a line to match the noun to the correct pronoun. The first one has been done for you.**

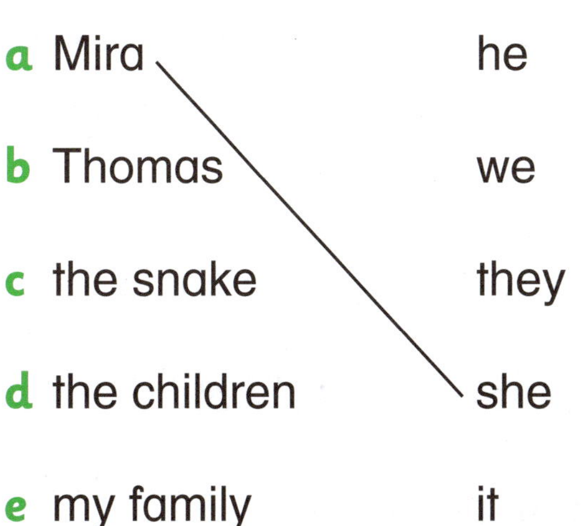

a Mira	he
b Thomas	we
c the snake	they
d the children	she
e my family	it

5 Use indirect speech to answer these questions about the diary.

a What did the captain of the boat say about the whales?

He said that ______________________________

______________________________.

b What did the tour guide say about coral?

She said that ______________________________

______________________________.

6 Circle the noun and matching pronoun in each pair of sentences. The first one has been done for you.

a (Yusef) goes swimming every Monday. (He) is in a squad with three other swimmers.

b Melbourne is a big city. It is the capital of Victoria.

c My class is going on an excursion. We are going to the zoo.

7 Draw a smiley face next to the sentences that are examples of indirect speech. Remember that indirect speech does not use speech marks (“ ”).

a “Come straight home after school,” said Mum to Jack.

b Mum told Jack to come straight home after school.

c Dad said that it looked as though it might rain.

8 **Rewrite the sentences. Replace the underlined nouns with pronouns. The first one has been done for you.**

a <u>Nick and Beth</u> are going to the shop.

They are going to the shop.

b <u>Dad</u> bought me a new pair of shoes.

____

c <u>Kimika</u> went to the skate park.

____

9 **Write a diary entry about something exciting you have done. Remember to use pronouns and indirect speech.**

____

____

____

____

____

____

____

____

Unit 9 Read All About It!

A **noun group** is a group of words that tells us more about a noun.

A **number adjective** tells how many of a noun there are, or in which order they come, for example *six pens*, *the third child*.

An **article** is a small word that comes before a noun, for example *a girl*, *an ape* or *the teacher*.

Newspaper Report

THE GLOBE

2 February

Hero dog saves owner!

A loyal pet saved its owner today in Petsville.

Late last night, a fire broke out at the home of 53-year-old Michael Sacco. Mr Sacco's dog, Richo, sounded the alarm.

First, Richo jumped over the back fence. The second thing he did was bark loudly. Third, he scraped his claws on a neighbour's back door.

Mr Sacco's neighbour heard the noise. She phoned 000.

"What an awful night. I owe my life to Richo," said a thankful Mr Sacco.

Richo's reward was a huge bone.

1 **Circle the number adjectives in the newspaper report in red.**

2 **Circle the articles in the newspaper report in blue. Use the words in the box to help you.**

the a an

3 **Underline two noun groups in the newspaper report. An example has been done for you.**

4 **Write the numbers 1–5 to show the order in which things happened. The first one has been done for you.**

- [ ] Richo barked loudly.
- [ ] The neighbour rang for help.
- [ ] Richo scraped his claws on the neighbour's back door.
- [1] The fire started.
- [ ] Richo jumped over the back fence.

5 **Write the adjectives and nouns in the correct columns of the table. The first one has been done for you.**

a thankful Mr Sacco

b loyal pet

c brave dog

d back fence

e local fire brigade

Adjectives	Nouns
thankful	Mr Sacco

6 **Choose an article, an adjective and a noun from each box to write noun groups. The first one has been done for you.**

Articles	Adjectives			Nouns	
the	blue	sweet	angry	lollies	dog
an	funny	brave	clever	boy	clown
a	fast	big	old	shoes	car

a the funny clown

b ____________________

c ____________________

d ____________________

e ____________________

7 **Write noun groups that include number adjectives to describe the pictures. The first one has been done for you.**

a three delicious cupcakes

b ____________________

c ____________________

d ____________________

8 Write a newspaper report. Use the picture and the headline to help you. Remember to include noun groups with articles and adjectives.

Boy finds hidden treasure

9 Read over your newspaper report. Write three noun groups you used in your newspaper report in the spaces below.

a ______________________________

b ______________________________

c ______________________________

Unit 10 Coin Cleaner

Technical nouns are nouns that relate to a special subject.

An **experiment** is a test to find out something. Experiments use many technical nouns, such as *equipment* and *results*.

Experiment

Coin cleaner

Aim

To see if a salt and vinegar mixture can clean old coins that look dirty.

Equipment

- a small bowl
- vinegar
- salt
- some old, dirty coins

Procedure

1 Pour some vinegar and salt into the bowl. Stir.

2 Put the coins into the mixture. Wait for 20 seconds.

3 Take out the coins and rinse them in water.

Results

The old, dirty coins are now shiny and clean.

The salt and vinegar mixture removes the dirt from the coins.

1 **Underline the headings in the experiment. The first one has been done for you.**

2 **Circle the technical nouns in the experiment. Use the words in the box to help you.**

mixture equipment results procedure aim

3 **Write the missing technical nouns.**

a The ______________ of the experiment is to see if a salt and vinegar ______________ can clean old coins that look dirty.

b Follow the steps in the ______________.

c Write the ______________ of the experiment after the procedure.

4 **Draw a line to match the technical noun to its definition. The first one has been done for you.**

a results	the things needed to do an experiment
b procedure	a liquid that is an acid
c mixture	what happened in an experiment
d vinegar	two or more things mixed together
e equipment	the steps that need to be done in an experiment

5 Circle the technical nouns in the sentences.

a The lion hunts for food. It is a predator.

b Ice is a solid, water is a liquid and steam is a gas.

c I clicked my mouse to start the game.

6 Write the missing headings in the experiment. Use the words in the box to help you.

Aim	Results	Procedure	Equipment

Vinegar volcano

____

To see what happens when you mix vinegar (an acid) with baking soda (a base).

____

- a small bowl
- vinegar
- baking soda

1 Put some baking soda into a bowl.

2 Pour some vinegar into the bowl.

____

The mixture fizzes up and spills out of the bowl.

7 **The table shows the results of an experiment to find out which objects will sink and which will float when placed in a bowl of water.**

Object	Float	Sink
table tennis ball	yes	no
spoon	no	yes
stone	no	yes
cork	yes	no

a Write one thing that floats in water. ______________________

b Write two things that sink in water.

______________________ ______________________

c Write the equipment you would need to do this experiment.

______________________ ______________________

______________________ ______________________

______________________ ______________________

8 **Write *yes* or *no* in the table below to say if you think each object floats or sinks in water.**

Object	Float	Sink
feather		
seashells		
beach ball		
shoe		

Unit 11 There Once Was ...

An **action verb** is a word that shows what is being done or what has been done – it is a *doing* word.
The mouse ran up the clock.

A **limerick** is funny poem with five lines that rhyme. Rhyme means that the last sound in every pair of lines sounds similar.

Limericks

Two Limericks

There once was a girl named Kate,
who wanted to learn how to skate.
So she tried and she tried,
but, oh, how she cried,
when she rolled and smashed into the gate.

Deep in the woods of McGunny,
was a bear who was searching for honey.
He found a beehive,
but the bees were alive.
So the bear had to give them his money.

1 **Circle the action verbs in the limericks. Use the words in the box to help you. Two have been done for you.**

wanted	rolled	learn	tried	smashed
cried	searching	give	found	skate

2 **Underline three rhyming words in the limericks. Three have been done for you.**

3 **Read the limericks aloud. Clap each time you hear a word that rhymes.**

4 **Draw a line to match the words that rhyme. The first one has been done for you.**

a cat — hay

b play — rake

c cake — hat

5 **Find the action verbs in the word search.**

cry   run   kiss   learn   sleep

j	s	s	c	r	y
s	l	x	r	u	s
n	e	y	p	n	s
l	e	a	r	n	i
m	p	c	m	i	k

6 Number the lines from the limerick to put them in the correct order. The first one has been done for you.

[ ] But on the day of the race,

[1] There once was a boy named Nash,

[ ] he was not in first place,

[ ] because he was sick with a rash.

[ ] who was fast like a lightning flash.

7 Use words from the box to fill in the gaps in the limericks. Some examples have been done for you.

~~kangaroo~~	~~Spain~~	"Ah-ah-choo!"	sheep	~~zoo~~
rain	sleep	didgeridoo	blew	~~again~~

There once was a young man from ___Spain___,

who went for a walk in the ______.

But the wind really ______,

And he sneezed, ______

So he had to go back home ___again___.

There once was a big ___kangaroo___,

who loved playing the ______.

But his friends couldn't ______,

though they tried counting ______.

So they sent kangaroo to the ___zoo___.

8 **Limericks have rhyming words in them. Think of rhyming words for these names.**

a Dan ______

b Jack ______

c Mary ______

d Sam ______

e Glen ______

f Ling ______

9 **Write an action verb to describe each picture.**

a

b

c

______ ______ ______

10 **Use your action verbs from activity 9 to write a sentence about each picture.**

a ______

b ______

c ______

Unit 12 Barry Bunny

An **antonym** is a word that is opposite in meaning to another word, for example *hot / cold, young / old*.

A **narrative** tells a story. There is a **sequence of events** that tells us the order in which things happen in a story.

This narrative is written as a poem with rhyming words.

Narrative – Rhyme

The Tale of Barry Bunny

Barry Bunny thought that he was big and strong and tough.
But his sister called him "gentle", and Barry had enough.
At the river he heard some screaming, some crying and a splash.
Sister Bunny was in trouble! Barry Bunny had to dash.

He grabbed a stick and held it out and leaned over the water.
"Grab on to this," he yelled to Sis and, just in time, he caught her.
At home again he said, "See? I'm big and brave and strong.
I'm not too small or scared or weak. I knew it, all along!"

1 **Circle the antonym for the word *big* in the rhyme.**

2 **Underline the antonym for the word *strong* in the rhyme.**

3 **Draw a line to match the word to its antonym. The first one has been done for you.**

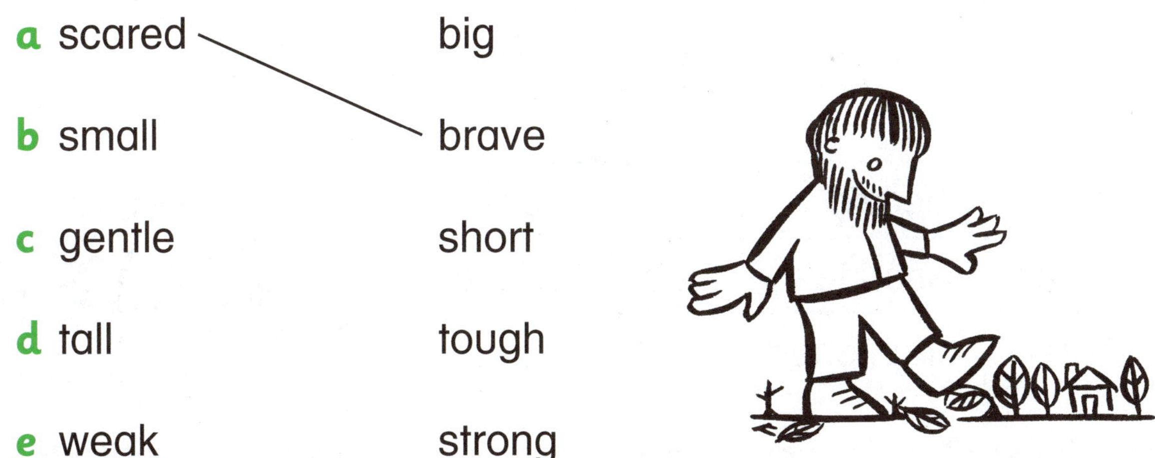

a scared	big
b small	brave
c gentle	short
d tall	tough
e weak	strong

4 **Number the sentences to show the correct sequence of events from the rhyme. The first one has been done for you.**

☐ Barry's sister is in trouble in the water.

☐ Barry catches and saves his sister.

☐ Barry hears his sister screaming by the river.

☐ Barry holds out a stick for his sister to grab.

1 Barry's sister calls him "gentle".

5 **Write an antonym for each word.**

a old ______________ b go ______________

c front ______________ d loud ______________

6 **Circle the antonym for each word in the table. The first one has been done for you.**

Word	Which is the antonym?		
sad	angry	(happy)	scared
new	young	fresh	old
pretty	beautiful	nice	ugly
big	tiny	large	enormous
strong	heavy	hard	weak
asleep	snoring	tired	awake
scared	frightened	lonely	brave

7 **Rewrite each sentence, replacing the underlined word with its antonym. Use the words in the box to help you. The first one has been done for you.**

~~worst~~ off dirty loses

a The <u>best</u> book I ever read was *Jumping Joe*.

The worst book I ever read was Jumping Joe.

b Our softball team usually <u>wins</u>.

____

c Can you turn <u>on</u> the TV?

____

d The dog is very <u>clean</u>.

____

8 **Write two pairs of antonyms you have learned today.**

9 **Write a short narrative to describe the sequence of events in these pictures.**

Unit 13 Frog Princess

A **conjunction** is a joining word. It connects parts of a sentence. *And*, *or*, *but*, *so* and *yet* are examples of conjunctions.

A **compound sentence** is made up of two or more simple sentences that can be linked by a conjunction.
My sister ate cake, but I ate biscuits.

Fairytale

The Dancing Frog Princess

Once upon a time there was a frog princess. She loved to dance, but she wanted someone to dance with.

One day a handsome frog visited her pond. He saw the princess and fell in love. He longed to talk to her, yet he was too shy.

Suddenly, the handsome frog sneezed. The princess turned. The frog didn't speak, so the princess turned away.

"I must speak now, or I will lose her forever," thought the frog. "May I have this dance?" he asked.

The frog princess smiled and took the handsome frog's hand for a dance.

They lived happily ever after.

1 **Underline three compound sentences in the fairytale. An example has been done for you.**

2 **Circle the conjunctions in the compound sentences. The first one has been done for you.**

a She loved to dance, (but) she wanted someone to dance with.

b He longed to talk to her, yet he was too shy.

c The frog didn't speak, so the princess turned away.

d "I must speak now, or I will lose her forever," thought the frog.

e The frog princess smiled and took the handsome frog's hand for a dance.

3 **Find the conjunctions in the word search.**

and but or yet because so

a	c	y	t	p	s	i	h
n	f	g	t	w	o	r	l
d	z	n	b	u	t	x	m
x	b	c	g	y	e	t	e
r	d	m	k	i	v	b	t
b	e	c	a	u	s	e	p

4 Draw a smiley face next to the compound sentences.

a I like to ride my bike, but I also like to ride my horse.

b My bike is very fast.

c Main Street was busy, so we went along Bridge Road.

d Main Street was very busy.

5 Fill in the gaps with the correct conjunctions. Use the words in the box to help you. The first one has been done for you.

a Our basketball team is good but my sister's team is better.

b It was snowing, ____________ we went skiing.

c Is this book my brother's, ____________ is it my sister's?

d I turned on the radio ____________ heard my favourite song.

6 Rewrite the simple sentences to make one compound sentence. Use the conjunctions in the box to help you. The first one has been done for you.

~~but~~ so yet

a I would eat vegetables. I don't like them.

I would eat vegetables, but I don't like them.

b The girl didn't want to go to school. She went anyway.

____

c The house was dirty. Cinderella cleaned it.

7 Write your own fairytale, or retell one you know. Here are some fairytales you could write about.

- *Snow White and the Seven Dwarfs*
- *The Pied Piper of Hamelin*
- *Rapunzel*

Once upon a time,

Unit 14 Hopscotch

A **connective** is a word or group of words that joins ideas in a text. *I am tired. However, I will still play.* Connectives are often placed at the beginning of a sentence. They help to **sequence actions** in time. *First, wash your hands. Then knead the dough.*

Game Instructions

Let's play hopscotch!

You will need:

- a flat, concrete area outside
- chalk
- a stone

How to play:

1 Use the chalk to draw a hopscotch grid.

2 To begin, throw your stone onto square number one. Your stone must land in the box.

3 Then hop over the square, and hop in the other squares to the end of the grid.

4 Next, turn around and hop back to square number two.

5 Now pick up your stone. Then hop over square number one.

6 Next, throw your stone onto square number two and hop again.

1 **Circle the connectives in the instructions in red. Use the words in the box to help you.**

next then to begin now

2 **Circle the first thing you need to do to play hopscotch in blue. Underline what you do second.**

3 **Find the connectives in the word search.**

first then next now however

f	r	t	h	e	n	y	p
i	d	t	n	m	w	j	k
r	d	t	x	e	n	j	q
s	h	o	w	e	v	e	r
t	c	v	h	w	o	n	l

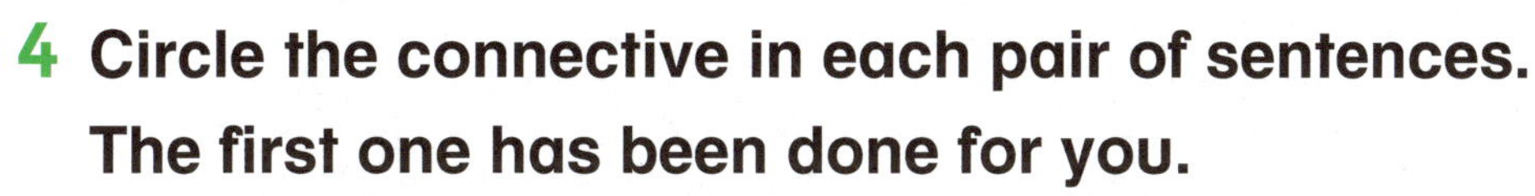

4 **Circle the connective in each pair of sentences. The first one has been done for you.**

a I am afraid of heights. However, I am going for a ride in a hot-air balloon.

b Put the flour and sugar in the bowl. Then add the egg and mix the ingredients together.

c I have done my reading and spelling homework. Next, I have to practise my times tables.

5 Fill in the gaps with the correct connectives. Use the words in the box to help you. The first one has been done for you.

~~To begin~~	However	For example

a We have lots of housework to do today. To begin, let's wash the dishes.

b Owning a kitten is a lot of work. __________, you need to feed it and change its kitty litter.

c Your drawing is looking good. __________, it still isn't finished.

6 Number the steps in the procedure so that the actions are done in the correct order. Use the pictures to help you.

1

2

3

4

_______ Next, use a pencil to draw a picture on the paper.

_______ Now stick your picture up on a wall.

_______ Then paint your picture.

_______ To begin, put a piece of paper on an easel.

 7 Write your own game instructions. Remember to use numbers to show the sequence of actions. Use connectives you have learned today to join the ideas together.

Let's play ____________________!

You will need:

- ____________________
- ____________________
- ____________________
- ____________________

How to play:

____

____

____

____

____

____

____

Unit 15 Cinquains

A **synonym** is a word that has the same or a similar meaning to another word, for example *cute / pretty*, *nice / kind*.

Some poems have a certain number of **syllables**, or beats, per line.

Cinquains

A cinquain is a poem with five lines.

- Line 1 = 2 syllables
- Line 2 = 4 syllables
- Line 3 = 6 syllables
- Line 4 = 8 syllables
- Line 5 = 2 syllables

Kitten

Cute and fluffy

Purring, prancing, sleeping ☆

A little ball of energy ☺

Small cat

Tiger

Fierce, stripy, strong

Stalking, creeping, pouncing

Silent hunter in the jungle

Big cat

The sun

Bright, hot, yellow

Shining, scorching, burning

We depend on your warmth and light

Our star

1 Circle the lines in the cinquains that have two syllables. The first one has been done for you.

2 Underline the lines in the cinquains that have four syllables. The first one has been done for you.

3 Draw a star next to the lines in the cinquains that have six syllables. The first one has been done for you.

4 Draw a smiley face next to the lines in the cinquains that have eight syllables. The first one has been done for you.

5 Draw a line to match the word to its synonym. The first one has been done for you.

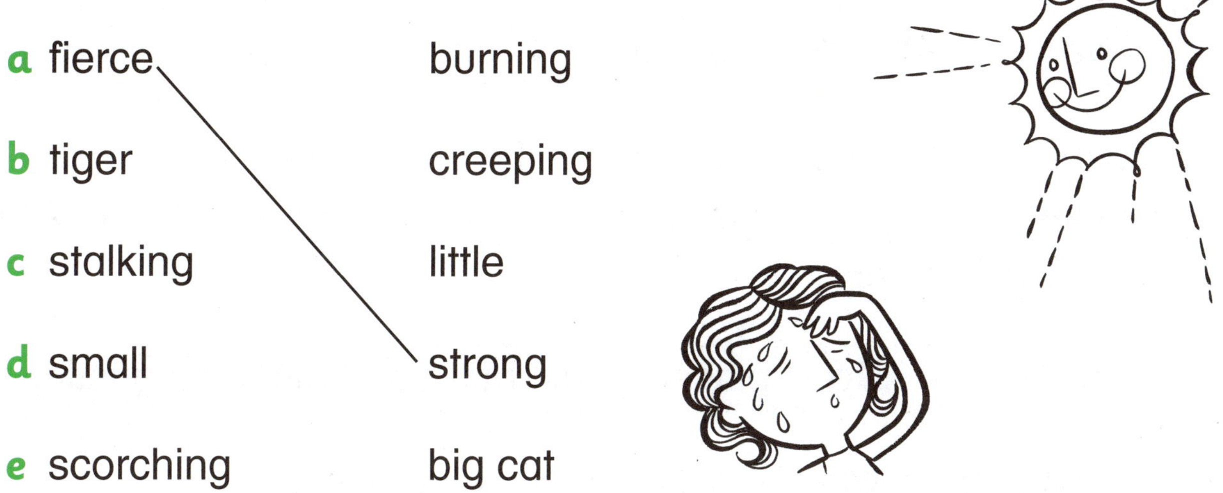

a fierce	burning
b tiger	creeping
c stalking	little
d small	strong
e scorching	big cat

6 Write a synonym for each word. The first one has been done for you.

a thin skinny

b stone ____________

c cheeky ____________

d chilly ____________

7 **Circle the synonym for each word in the table. The first one has been done for you.**

Word	Which is the synonym?		
happy	sad	angry	(cheerful)
small	big	enormous	little
tasty	delicious	horrible	disgusting
hungry	thirsty	full	starving
child	adult	kid	woman
laugh	cry	funny	giggle
sleep	awake	tired	snooze
dance	boogie	walk	run
river	stream	ocean	lake

8 **Rewrite each sentence, replacing the underlined word with its synonym. Use the words in the box to help you. The first one has been done for you.**

~~amusing~~ like placed exhausted gift disgusting

a It was <u>funny</u> when the clown fell in the water.

It was amusing when the clown fell in the water.

b This pizza is <u>terrible</u>!

____

c I was <u>tired</u> after my basketball game.

____

d Chen and Debbie enjoy dancing.

____

e I put her present on the table.

____

9 Write your own cinquain.

Step 1: Think of a person, animal or thing you would like to write a cinquain about. This is the subject of your cinquain.

Step 2: Write the subject of your cinquain in the space provided.

Step 3: Write your cinquain.

Remember that each line has a certain number of syllables.

Use the information below to help you.

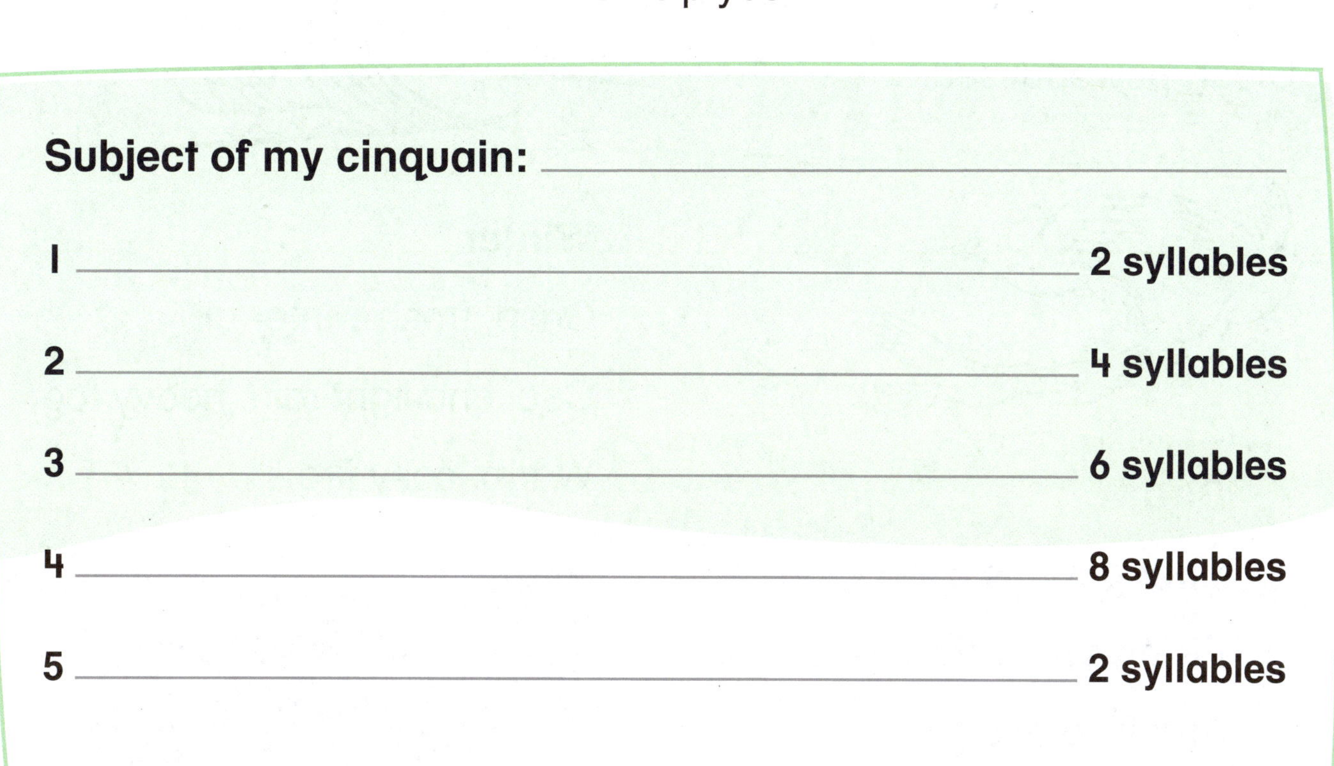

Subject of my cinquain: ______________________________

1 ______________________________ **2 syllables**

2 ______________________________ **4 syllables**

3 ______________________________ **6 syllables**

4 ______________________________ **8 syllables**

5 ______________________________ **2 syllables**

Unit 16 All About Nature

Descriptive language uses words that tell us about things. An **adjective** is a word that tells us more about a noun.

The car was big, fast and new.

Adjectives can also be numbers that tell us how many or how much, for example *three cars.*

Haiku

A haiku is a type of poem. It is made up of three lines:

- Line 1 = 5 syllables
- Line 2 = 7 syllables
- Line 3 = 5 syllables

The Sea

Salty, crashing waves
Blue, green water meeting sand
Clear, powerful sea

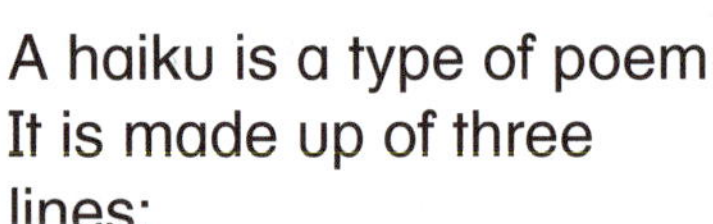

Winter

Crisp, fresh winter air
Cool and light rain, heavy fog
Warm, cosy fire

Bird

Strong wings open wide,
Flying swiftly through the air
Amazing bird glides

1 Write the adjectives used in the haiku to describe these nouns. The first one has been done for you.

a Salty, crashing waves

b ____________, ____________ water

c ____________ and ____________ rain

d ____________ fog

e ____________, ____________ fire

2 Underline the lines in the haiku that have five syllables.

3 Write two adjectives to describe each picture. The first one has been done for you.

a pretty, bright

b ____________, ____________

c ____________, ____________

d ____________, ____________

4 **Write the number adjectives in this haiku.**

Five pretty school girls,

Skipping around the playground

Ten small hands clapping

____

5 **Write a sentence using the adjectives listed. The first one has been done for you.**

a smelly, brown, two

The two smelly brown boots have to stay outside.

b five, pink

____

c yellow, two

____

d round, one, bouncy

____

6 **Write a descriptive sentence about this picture. Remember to use adjectives.**

____

____

7 **Write two descriptive sentences using adjectives and nouns from the table.**

Adjectives			Nouns		
big	fast	quiet	horse	car	tiger
stripy	young	green	hat	house	jumper

____

____

8 **Write your own haiku.**

Step 1: Think of something from nature that you would like to write a haiku about. This is the subject of your haiku.

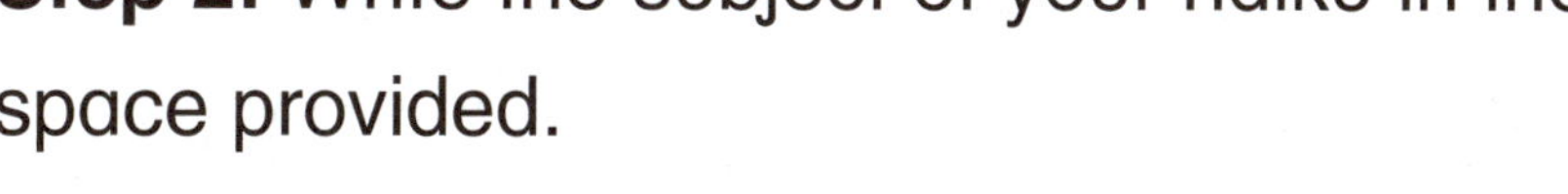

Step 2: Write the subject of your haiku in the space provided.

Step 3: Write your haiku.

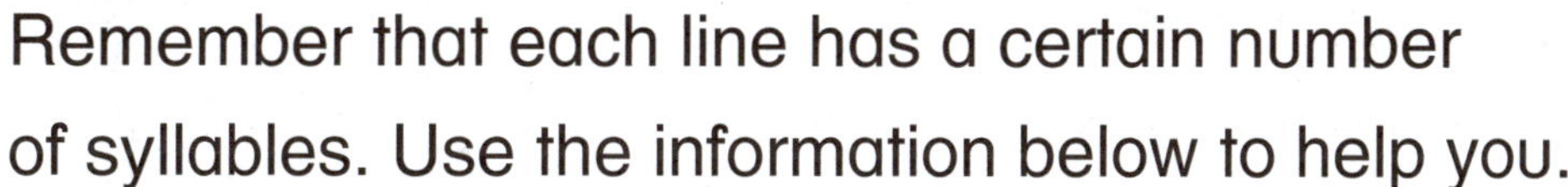

Remember that each line has a certain number of syllables. Use the information below to help you.

Subject of my haiku: ______________________________

1 ______________________________ **5 syllables**

2 ______________________________ **7 syllables**

3 ______________________________ **5 syllables**

Unit 17 Planting Day

A **statement of fact** is a sentence that gives us true information. A **statement of opinion** shows someone's judgement or view about something.

An **exclamation mark** (!) is a punctuation mark used to show surprise, shock or joy. *I can't believe we won!*

Advertisement

Community Planting Day

We need your help!

When: Saturday 15 August – all day!

Where: Fraser Wetlands,
22 Garden Grove, Fraserville

Bring: Gardening gloves,
sun hat, sunscreen

<u>We have over 1000 plants that need to be planted.</u> The plants will make the wetlands healthy, and will provide a home for native animals.

Our planting day will be a fun day for everyone! ☆

This is a very important project!

Free sausage sizzle! Face painting for kids! Local crafts for sale!

1 **Underline one statement of fact in the advertisement. An example has been done for you.**

2 **Draw a star next to one statement of opinion in the advertisement. An example has been done for you.**

3 **Circle the exclamation marks in the advertisement.**

4 **Draw a smiley face next to the statement of fact in each pair of sentences.**

a My brother plays guitar.
My brother doesn't practise enough.

b My cousin's horse is the fastest in the stable!
My cousin owns a horse.

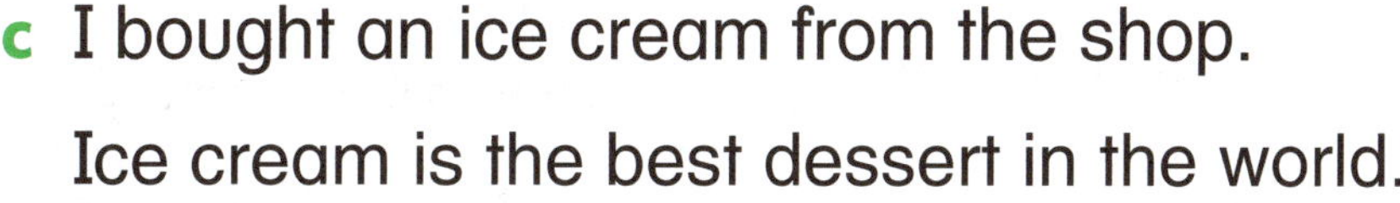

c I bought an ice cream from the shop.
Ice cream is the best dessert in the world.

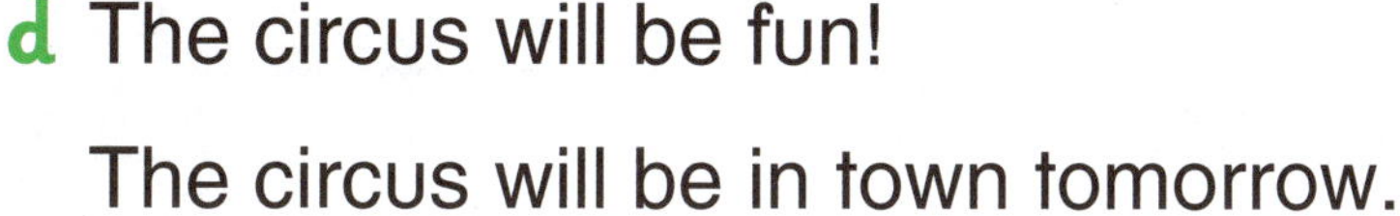

d The circus will be fun!
The circus will be in town tomorrow.

5 **Write exclamation marks or full stops where you think they are needed to finish these sentences.**

a I will go to bed soon

b I can't wait to go to the snow

c Wow, look at that aeroplane

d My pencil needs sharpening

6 **Write a sentence that tells us something exciting about each picture. Use an exclamation mark.**

a ______________________________

____

b ______________________________

____

c ______________________________

____

7 **Write an F for Fact or an O for Opinion next to the sentences. The first one has been done for you.**

a The girls are playing with a ball. F

b The man really needs this holiday. ___

c The man has two daughters. ___

d The man is wearing sunglasses. ___

e Swimming is a great thing to do on a holiday. ___

f The man is lying on a lounge chair. ___

g It would be fun to play in the pool. ___

8 Write a statement of fact or a statement of opinion about each picture.

a Fact: ______________________

____

b Opinion: ______________________

____

9 Write an advertisement of your own. Remember to include exclamation marks and draw suitable pictures. Here are some topics you could write about.

- A carnival
- A concert
- A school play

Unit 18

The Canoe Tree

A **question** is a sentence used to find out information or ask for something.

Are you going to school tomorrow?

Questions always end with a **question mark** (?).

Explanation

The Canoe Tree

What is a canoe tree?

A canoe tree is a tree, often a gum tree, with a large "scar" on its trunk. In the past, Aboriginal peoples would cut a large piece of bark from a tree, and use it to make a canoe.

How was the bark removed?

Stone axes were used to loosen the bark. Then it was carefully pulled from the tree.

How were the canoes made?

The bark was put over hot coals. The heat made the sides of the bark curl up. The bark could be bent into shape. Then the edges were strengthened with clay.

1 **Circle the question marks in the explanation.**

2 **Underline the questions in the explanation.**

3 **Draw a line to match the question to its correct answer. The first one has been done for you.**

a Do you like horses? ————	Yes, I do like horses.
b When is the concert?	Polar bears live in the Arctic Circle.
c Do you have a sister?	My name is Milly.
d Where do polar bears live?	The concert is next week.
e What is your name?	No, I don't have a sister.

4 **Write question marks at the end of the sentences that are questions. Write full stops at the end of the sentences that are not questions.**

a Where is the party____

b I would like some cake, please____

c May I have some cake, please____

d What did you get for your birthday____

e I got a new bike for my birthday____

5 **Where does a question mark go?**

A question mark goes ______________________________.

6 **Write a question about each picture. Remember to use a question mark. Use the words in the box to help you. The first one has been done for you.**

where how what when why which

a What is the monkey eating?

b ______________________________

____

c ______________________________

____

d ______________________________

____

e ______________________________

____

7 Write your own explanation. Include questions and remember to use question marks. Here are some topics you could write about.

- Your favourite sport
- An animal
- Outer space

Title: ______________________________

Question: ______________________________

Answer: ______________________________

____

____

Question: ______________________________

Answer: ______________________________

____

____

Question: ______________________________

Answer: ______________________________

____

____

Unit 19 Going Green

A **statement of fact** gives us true information about something.

Past tense verbs are verbs that tell us about actions that have already happened. Examples of past tense verbs are *planted, used* and *said*.

Newspaper Report

THE GLOBE

17 August

Going green a huge success!

On Saturday 15 August, people from Fraserville attended a community planting day. They planted over 1000 plants in the Fraser Wetlands.

"We planted species that are native to Australia," said Kevin Dudley, the organiser of the day. "Many of these plant species were used once by local Aboriginal peoples. They used the plants for food and medicine. They also weaved baskets and made jewellery from the plants."

The day was a huge success and the plants will help make the wetlands lush and healthy.

1 **Circle the past tense verbs in the newspaper report. Use the words in the box to help you.**

made used weaved was
were planted attended said

2 **Complete the statements of fact. Use the information in the newspaper report to help you.**

a The Fraserville planting day was held on Saturday ________________ August.

b The community planted over ________________ plants.

c They planted species that are native to ________________.

d Local Aboriginal peoples weaved ________________ and made ________________ from the plants.

e The organiser of the planting day was ________________ ________________.

3 **Circle the past tense verbs in the sentences.**

a The baby said her first word.

b I made a delicious chocolate cake.

c They all went to the movies.

d She swam faster than ever.

4 **Write the past tense verbs for these words. The first one has been done for you.**

a kick kicked ________ b plant ________

c make ________ d use ________

5 **Write a statement of fact about each picture. The first one has been done for you.**

a Kangaroos carry their babies in their pouches.

b ________________________________

c ________________________________

d ________________________________

6 **Fill in the gaps with the correct past tense verbs. Use the words in the box to help you.**

planted	went	did	played	spent	bought

Last weekend, I ________ to stay with my grandparents.

We ________ lots of fun things together!

On Saturday, Grandpa and I ______________ some plants at a plant shop. Later, Grandma and I ______________ the plants in the garden.

We ______________ Sunday afternoon at the park. I ______________ on the swings and the slide.

7 Write a short recount of an event that happened in the past. Draw a picture to go with your recount.

____

____

____

____

____

____

Unit 20 Feed Me!

A **concrete noun** is something that can be touched, seen or heard. Examples of concrete nouns are *car*, *ice* and *song*.

Precise language includes sentences that are short, clear and easy to understand.

Venn Diagram

Carnivores, Herbivores and Omnivores

Animals that eat only meat are called *carnivores*.

Animals that eat only plants are called *herbivores*.

Animals that eat both meat and plants are called *omnivores*.

This Venn diagram shows examples of animals that are carnivores, herbivores and omnivores.

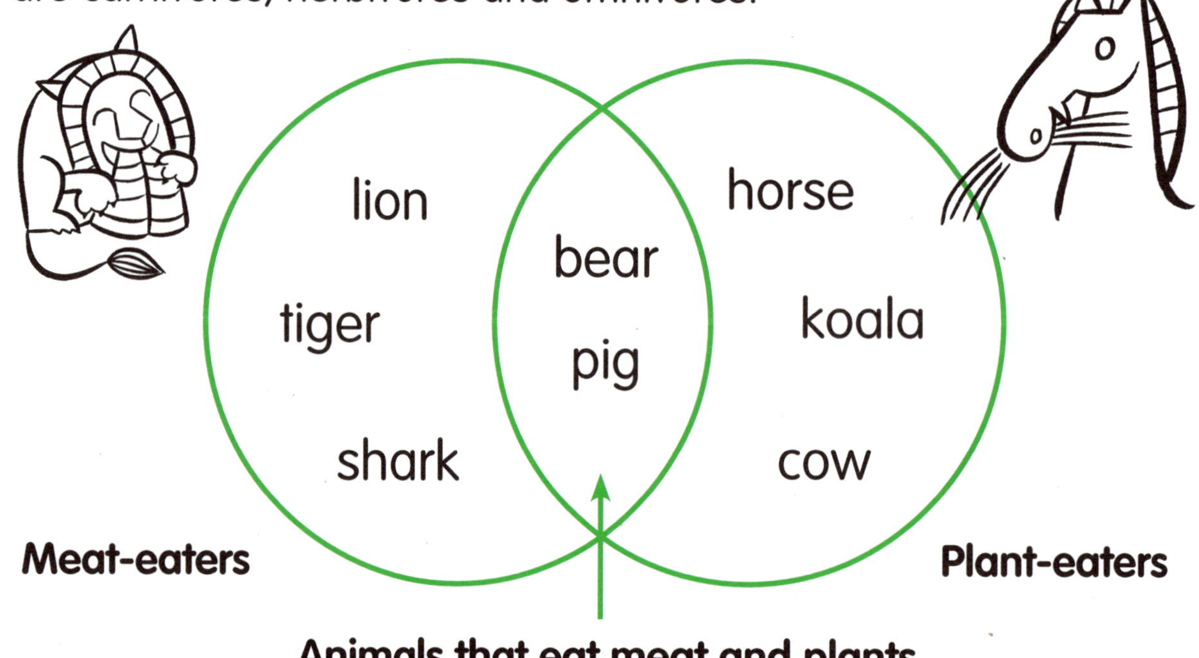

1 **Write the name of an animal that only eats meat.** ____________

2 **Write the name of an animal that only eats plants.** ____________

3 **Write the name of an animal that eats both meat and plants.**

____

4 **Circle the sentences that are precise. Remember, precise sentences are short, clear and easy to understand.**

a Thank you for not smoking.

b The bright pink flower opened slowly as the sunlight came through the open window.

c My house is the smallest in the street.

5 **Find the concrete nouns in the word search.**

lion tiger meat animal plant pig

x	q	p	t	l	p	w	t
t	i	g	e	r	i	n	a
d	t	a	n	m	e	t	e
s	a	n	i	m	a	l	m
g	i	p	b	l	i	o	n
s	d	p	l	a	n	t	l

6 Circle the sentence in each pair that is written in precise language. The first one has been done for you.

a Pigs eat meat, corn, wheat, oats and barley.

Pigs eat meat and plants. (circled)

b The clown did circus tricks.

The clown juggled balls and walked on a tightrope.

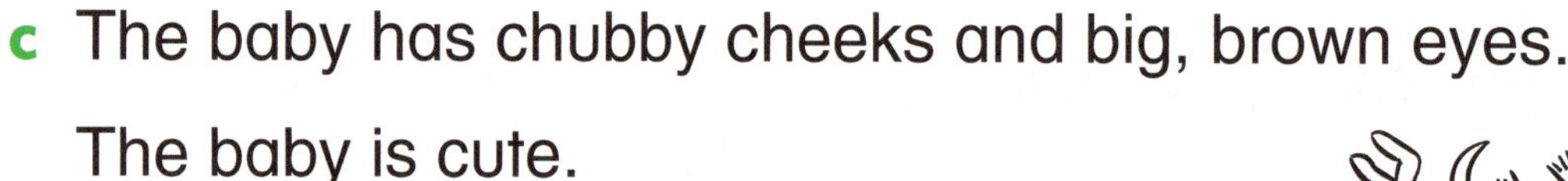

c The baby has chubby cheeks and big, brown eyes.

The baby is cute.

d The cat seemed scared.

The cat arched its back and hissed.

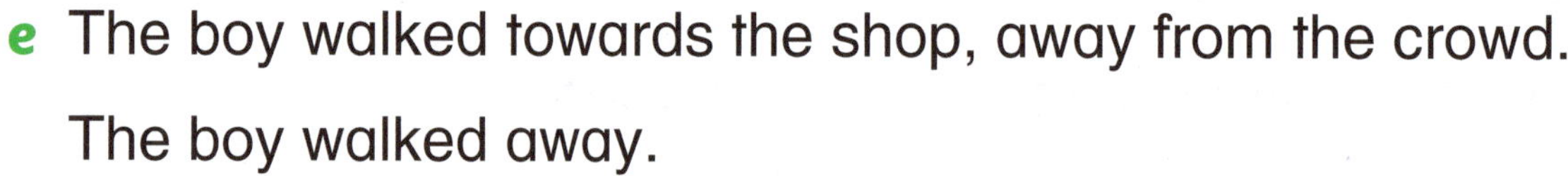

e The boy walked towards the shop, away from the crowd.

The boy walked away.

7 Circle the concrete nouns. An example has been done for you.

horse (circled)	hope	fork
strawberries	Tom	sympathy
bread	juice	anger
luck	shoes	piglet
humour	book	sadness

8 Write a precise sentence about one of the concrete nouns you have circled in activity 7.

9 Write a short story about a visit to a place you like to go. Remember to include concrete nouns that can be touched, seen or heard. Draw a picture to go with your story.

Unit 21 My Eyes

An **adverb** is a word that gives us extra information about a verb. It tells us where, when and how an action happens. Adverbs often end with the letters –ly, such as *happily*. Other adverbs are *yesterday*, *often* and *never*.

Explanation

How My Eyes Work

Diagram of the eye

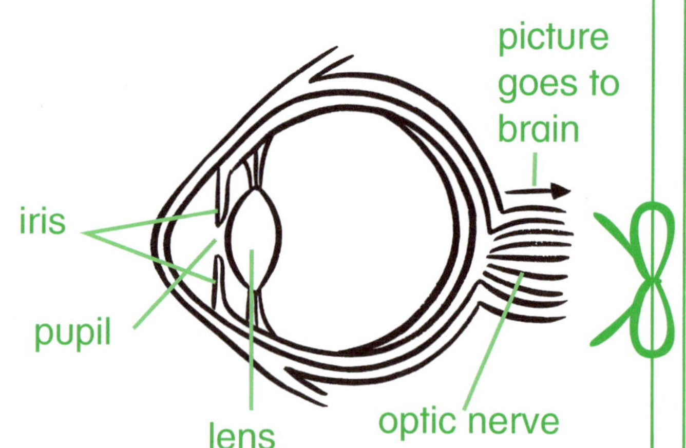

How do I see?

Light enters the pupil of the eye and quickly passes through to the lens. The lens puts a picture on the back of the eye. The picture talks to the brain.

Why do I blink?

Blinking protects the eyes. When something is in your eye you blink immediately to remove it. You blink when a bright light is turned on, or when something gets too close to your eye. People can blink rapidly – up to five times a second. We also blink often – on average about 15 blinks per minute.

1 **Circle the adverbs in the explanation. Use the words in the box to help you.**

quickly	often	rapidly	immediately

2 **Shade the lens in the diagram of the eye in green.**

3 **Shade the pupil in the diagram of the eye in blue.**

4 **Find the adverbs in the word search.**

quickly	rapidly	often	quietly	never

n	q	u	i	c	k	l	y
e	y	l	t	e	i	u	q
v	w	o	f	t	e	n	t
e	c	v	n	m	i	p	n
r	a	p	i	d	l	y	h

5 **Draw a line to match each question to its correct diagram.**

a What are the parts of a plant?

b What is the life cycle of a butterfly?

c Where is Australia?

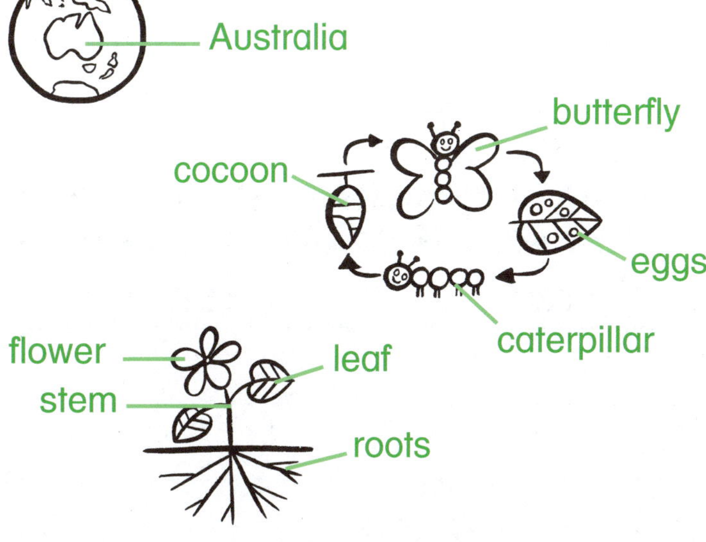

6 Circle the adverbs in each pair of words.

a loud loudly

b happy happily

c soft softly

d sadly sad

7 Fill in the gaps in each sentence with a verb and an adverb. The first one has been done for you.

Verbs		Adverbs	
~~drove~~	looked	~~slowly~~	heavily
rained	swim	everywhere	regularly

a The car drove slowly up the hill.

b I ______ ______ at the pool.

c I ______ ______ for my keys.

d It ______ ______ last winter.

8 Sort the adverbs in the box into the table. Some examples have been done for you.

~~here~~	~~today~~	~~quickly~~
yesterday	slowly	there
everywhere	never	loudly

WHERE adverbs	WHEN adverbs	HOW adverbs
here	today	quickly

9 **Write your own explanation. Draw a diagram to go with your explanation. Here are some topics you could write about.**

- How does it rain?
- How does a boat float?
- Why do we have day and night?

Unit 22 Sandcastles

A **synonym** is a word that has a similar meaning to another word, for example *sad / upset*.

An **antonym** is a word that has the opposite meaning to another word, for example *young / old.*

Direct speech is what someone says. Speech marks (“ ”) are used in direct speech. *“Hello Alice,” said Pip.*

Story

The Great Sandcastle Competition

Adam had never won a sandcastle competition. He was nervous. Adam’s brother Simon had won three. He was confident.

Adam built a fantastic sandcastle. It even had a tower. Suddenly, Adam felt water at his feet.

“The tide is coming in!” yelled Simon.

Adam’s sandcastle was destroyed. “It’s ruined!” he cried.

The judges announced that Simon was the winner.

Simon ran to collect the prize. He looked over and saw Adam’s sad face. Simon knew what to do.

“I am giving this prize to Adam,” he said. “His sandcastle was excellent!”

Adam was happy to have finally won.

1 **Underline the direct speech in the story. An example has been done for you.**

2 **Write a sentence of direct speech that Simon says in the story.**

____

3 **Draw a line to match the word to its synonym. The first one has been done for you.**

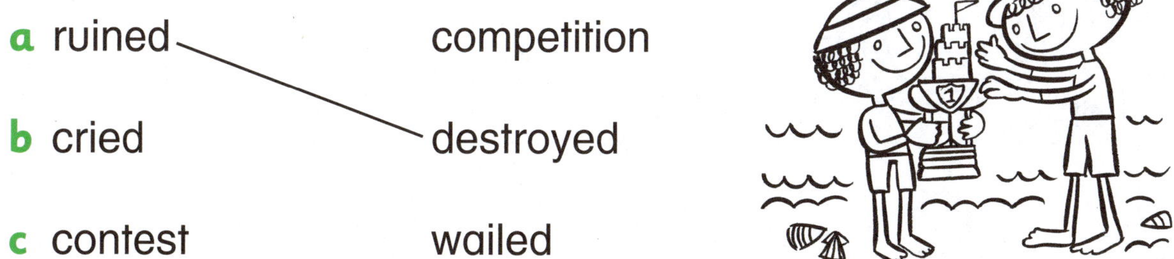

a ruined — competition

b cried — destroyed

c contest — wailed

4 **Draw a line to match the word to its antonym. The first one has been done for you.**

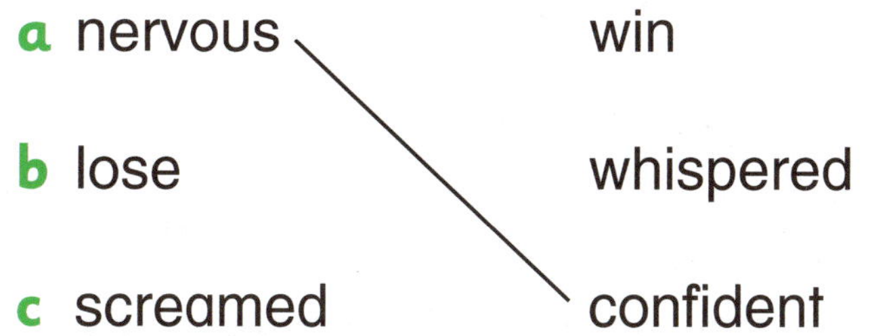

a nervous — win

b lose — whispered

c screamed — confident

5 **Circle the matching synonyms in each row of words. The first one has been done for you.**

a clown   funny   amusing   laugh

b learning   young   children   kids

c wet   rain   cold   soaked

d happy   smile   cheerful   cry

6 **Write a synonym and an antonym for the words in the table.**

	Synonym	Antonym
happy		
hot		
huge		
kind		

7 **Write speech marks in the correct places in these sentences. The first one has been done for you.**

a "I don't want to go to school!" yelled the boy.

b Goodnight, sweetheart, said Mum.

c Ha, ha! That movie was funny! said the girl.

d The music is really loud! shouted the man.

e Will you please be quiet! said the teacher.

8 **Write your own story. Remember to include direct speech. You can write about anything you like, but here are some topics you could write about.**

- A singing / talent competition
- A chess competition
- A video game competition

Title: ______________________________

____

____

____

____

____

____

____

____

____

Unit 23 The Letter Hunt

Commands tell someone to do or not to do something. *Give me that book! Don't do that!*

Conjunctions are words that join ideas together in a sentence. *It is cold, so I will put on my jacket.*

Directions

Miss Grey's Letter Hunt

Dear class,

I have made a letter hunt. I know you'll enjoy it, because you love puzzles so much.

Look at the map. Find the letters hidden around the school. The letters will spell a mystery word.

Have fun!

Miss Grey

1 Use the map to write the correct letters in the table.

	Directions	Letters
1	Go outside and look under the flagpole.	
2	Walk to the big gum tree.	
3	Go to the sandpit, but try not to get dirty.	
4	Look in the playground near the seesaw.	
5	Climb up to the slide, so you can reach the next letter.	
6	Look in the vegetable garden.	
7	Go into the tunnel. Keep your head low, or you might hit it!	

2 Circle the conjunctions in the directions above. Use the words in the box to help you.

and or so but

3 Underline the commands in the letter and in the directions. The first one has been done for you.

4 Circle the conjunctions in the sentences. The first one has been done for you.

a I want to buy a new scooter, (but) I don't have enough money.

b I want to take swimming lessons because I don't know how to swim.

c I'm tired, yet I can't sleep!

5 Underline the sentences that are commands. The first one has been done for you.

a <u>Eat your dinner!</u>

b Don't forget your hat!

c You ate all of your dinner.

d Pass the sugar, please.

e Play the guitar.

f May I have the salt, please?

6 Write a command for each verb. The first one has been done for you.

a take Please take your feet off the sofa!

b eat __________

c give __________

d walk __________

e tidy __________

7 Write a sentence for each conjunction. The first one has been done for you.

a because I eat vegetables because they're good for me.

b yet __________

____

c or __________

____

8 Write directions from your home to a place you go to often. Write simple commands, and draw a map to go with them. Here are some places you could write about.

- School
- Your local shops
- A swimming pool
- A skate park

Directions from home to ______________________________

____

____

____

____

____

____

Unit 24 My Dad, the Hero

A **present tense verb** tells us about an action that is happening now or happens regularly. *The lion eats meat.*

Present tense –ing verbs tell us about actions that are happening now, and actions that will continue for a while. *The lion is eating meat.*

A **statement of opinion** is someone's view about something.

Book Review

My Dad, the Hero

My Dad, the Hero, by Stella Gurney, is an excellent picture book.

The story is about a boy called Tariq. Tariq's teacher asks his dad to give a talk to the class. But Tariq's dad can't speak English. Tariq is proud of his dad, but he is worried. In the end, Tariq's dad gives a great presentation.

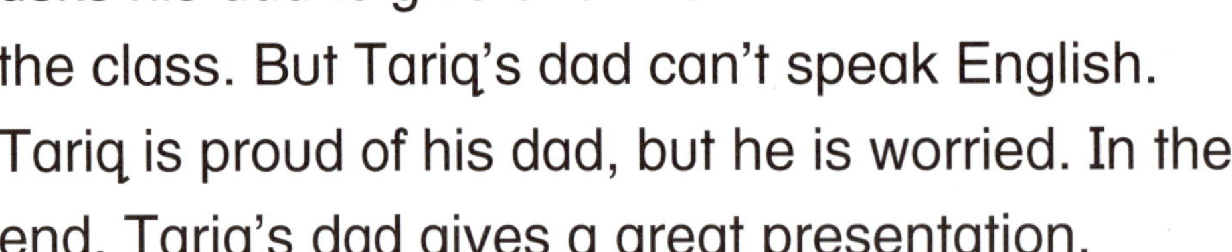

This book is very good. I am asking you to read it because it is really interesting. I have already told lots of people to read it. My sister is reading it right now. Read it – you'll love it!

1 **Circle the present tense verbs in the book review. Use the words in the box to help you.**

is asks give read gives speak love

2 **Underline the present tense –ing verbs in the book review. Use the words in the box to help you.**

asking reading

3 **Draw a smiley face next to a statement of opinion in the book review.**

4 **Fill in the gaps with the correct present tense –ing verbs. Use the words in the box to help you. The first one has been done for you.**

~~is swimming~~	is roaring
are playing	is singing

a The girl is swimming.

b The boy ______.

c The lion ______.

d The children ______.

5 **Rewrite these sentences to turn them into present tense –ing sentences. The first one has been done for you.**

a Mum cooks delicious food.

Mum is cooking delicious food.

b The princess wears a crown.

____

c I wait for the bus.

____

6 **Draw a smiley face beside the statement of opinion in each pair of sentences.**

a Sydney will win the AFL grand final this year.
Sydney has a football team in the AFL.

b I like to eat ice cream.
Ice cream is cold and sweet.

c Tricycles have three wheels.
Tricycles are fun to ride.

7 **Write a sentence of opinion about each picture.**

a

____

b

c

8 Write a book review about a book you have read recently. Remember to include the title of the book, the author's name and statements of opinion about the book.

Unit 25 The Class Party

An **abstract noun** a noun that cannot be seen, touched or heard. Examples of abstract nouns are *excitement* and *fun*.

Emotive language is used to make readers feel something, or to persuade readers of something. *It is our last chance.*

Invitation

Party Invitation

To 2D, the best class in the whole wide world!

I am moving to Adelaide next year. It is my pleasure to invite you to a farewell party.

Where: In our classroom

When: 14 December, at lunchtime

We will play games and sing songs. What excitement!

I will miss you all lots next year, but I will always remember the friendships I have made. Good luck next year!

I can't wait to see you at the party! It's going to be heaps of fun. Don't forget to bring your lunch.

From,

James

1 **Circle the abstract nouns in the invitation. Use the words in the box to help you.**

pleasure luck fun friendships excitement

2 **Underline a sentence in the invitation that uses emotive language. An example has been done for you.**

3 **Find the abstract nouns in the word search.**

pleasure joy luck fun peace

p	l	e	a	s	u	r	e
e	w	m	l	u	c	k	p
a	b	n	j	o	y	l	o
c	r	e	r	t	b	n	m
e	d	r	t	a	n	u	f

4 **Draw a smiley face next to the sentence in each pair that uses emotive language. The first one has been done for you.**

a Can you play soccer this weekend?
We need you in our soccer team! ☺

b The girl sobbed her heart out.
The girl cried.

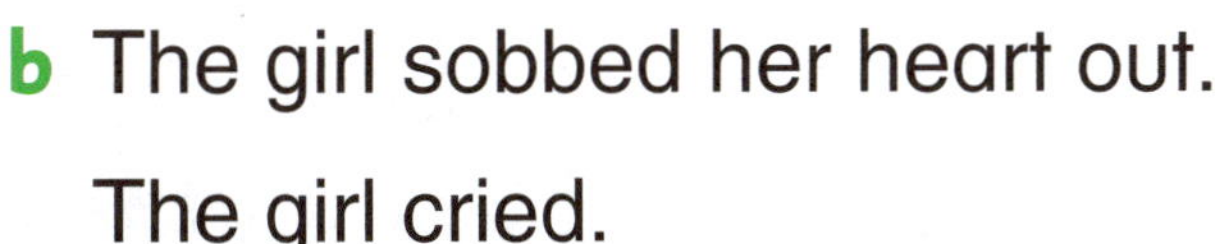

c The ocean was cold.
The ocean was so cold I almost froze!

5 **Write the nouns in the box in the correct column in the table. Some examples have been done for you.**

~~house~~	~~improvement~~	friendship
dog	sadness	bravery
rice	hunger	firefighter
frog	woman	anger

Concrete nouns	Abstract nouns
house	improvement

6 **Write a sentence about each picture. Use the abstract nouns in the box to help you.**

anger excitement fun

a ______________________________

b ______________________________

c ______________________________

 7 **Write an invitation for a party. Use emotive language and abstract nouns. Remember to include:**

- when and where the party will be
- what the party is for.

Party Invitation

Glossary

abstract noun	a noun that cannot be seen, touched or heard
action verb	a word that expresses doing or being
adjective	a word that describes a noun
adverb	a word that tells us more about a verb
antonym	a word that is opposite in meaning to another word
article	a small word that comes before a noun (e.g. a, an, the)
capital letter	a letter used at the start of a sentence and the start of a proper noun
cinquain	a poem with five lines and 22 syllables
collective noun	a noun that talks about a group of people or things
comma	a punctuation mark (,) used to separate thoughts and ideas
command	a sentence that tells someone to do or not to do something
compound sentence	a sentence made up of two or more simple sentences
concrete noun	a noun that can be touched, seen or heard
conjunction	a word used to link two ideas (e.g. and, but, so)
connective	a word or group of words that joins ideas in a text
descriptive language	language that uses words that tell us about things
dialogue	when two or more people talk to each other
direct speech	actual words spoken by the speaker; used within speech marks
dot point	a point that runs down a page to make a list
emotive language	words that try to make us feel something
exclamation mark	a punctuation mark (!) used to give emphasis or show surprise, shock or joy
experiment	a test to find out something
full stop	a punctuation mark (.) used to show the end of a sentence
haiku	a poem with three lines and 17 syllables
indirect speech	tells about what was said; not the actual spoken words
instruction	tells us how to make or do something
limerick	a funny poem with five lines that rhyme
narrative	a story
noun	a word that names people, places and things
noun group	a noun and a group of words that tells us more about the noun
number adjective	a word that tells us how many of a noun there are or their order
past tense	used to write about things that have already happened
precise language	language that uses words that are clear and to the point

present tense –ing verb	a word that tells us about an action that is happening now, and an action that will continue for a while
pronoun	a word that takes the place of a noun (e.g. I, you, we)
proper noun	the name of a person, place or thing
question	a sentence used to find out information or ask for something
question mark	a punctuation mark (?) used at the end of a question
sequence of events	tells us the order in which things happen
simple sentence	a group of words that contains a subject and a verb
statement of fact	a sentence that gives true information about something
statement of opinion	a sentence that shows someone's view or judgement
syllable	a part of a word that makes up a beat in a line of a poem
synonym	a word with the same or similar meaning to another word
technical noun	a noun that relates to a special subject
topic sentence	a sentence that tells us what a paragraph is about
verb	an action word that shows what is being done

This is to certify that

....

is a Grammar Guru

Signed ....

School ....

Date ....

GRAMMAR GURU